THE NATIONAL SOCIETY FOR PERFORMANCE AND INSTRUCTION (NSPI)

The National Society for Performance and Instruction (NSPI) is the leading international association dedicated to improving productivity and performance in the workplace. Founded in 1962, NSPI represents over ten thousand members throughout the United States and Canada and in thirty-three other countries. NSPI members work in over three thousand businesses, governmental agencies, academic institutions, and other organizations. Monthly meetings of over sixty different chapters provide professional development, services, and information exchange.

NSPI members include performance technologists, training directors, human resource managers, instructional technologists, human factors practitioners, and organizational development consultants. They are business executives, professors, line managers, government leaders, and military commanders. They work in a variety of areas: the armed forces, financial services, government agencies, health services, high technology, manufacturing, telecommunications, travel and hospitality, and universities. NSPI members are leaders in their fields and work settings. They are strategy-oriented, quality-focused, and results-centered.

The mission of NSPI is to improve the performance of individuals and organizations through the application of Human Performance Technology (HPT). NSPI's vision for itself is to be the preferred source of information, education, and advocacy for enhancing individual and organizational effectiveness, and to be respected for the tangible and enduring impact it is having on people, organizations, and the field of performance technology.

NSPI makes a difference to people by helping them grow into skilled professionals who use integrated and systematic approaches to add value to their organizations and the profession. Whether designing training programs, building selection or incentive systems, assisting organizations in their own re-design, or performing myriad other interventions, NSPI members produce results.

NSPI makes a difference to organizations by increasing professional competence and confidence. NSPI members help organizations anticipate opportunities and challenges and develop powerful solutions that contribute to productivity and satisfaction.

NSPI makes a difference to the field of performance technology by expanding the boundaries of what we know about defining, teaching, supporting, and maintaining skilled human performance. With a healthy respect for research and development, a variety of technologies, and collegial interaction, NSPI members use approaches and systems that ensure improved productivity and a better world.

For additional information, contact:

National Society for Performance and Instruction
1300 L Street, N.W., Suite 1250
Washington, DC 20005
Telephone: (202) 408-7969
Fax: (202) 408-7972

DESIGNING WORK GROUPS, JOBS, AND WORK FLOW

A PUBLICATION IN THE NSPI SERIES

From Training to Performance in the Twenty-First Century

Kenneth H. Silber, Series Editor

Titles in the Series

Set 1:
DESIGNING THE WORK ENVIRONMENT FOR OPTIMUM PERFORMANCE
Elaine Weiss, Topic Editor

CREATING THE ERGONOMICALLY SOUND WORKPLACE
Lee T. Ostrom

CREATING WORKPLACES WHERE PEOPLE CAN THINK
Phyl Smith and Lynn Kearny

MAKING COMPUTERS PEOPLE-LITERATE
Elaine Weiss

Set 2:
REDESIGNING WORK PROCESSES
Judith A. Hale, Topic Editor

DESIGNING WORK GROUPS, JOBS, AND WORK FLOW
Toni Hupp with Craig Polak and Odin Westgaard

DESIGNING CROSS-FUNCTIONAL BUSINESS PROCESSES
Bernard Johann

DESIGNING WORK GROUPS, JOBS, AND WORK FLOW

Toni Hupp

with

Craig Polak

and

Odin Westgaard

 **JOSSEY–BASS PUBLISHERS**
SAN FRANCISCO

Substantial discounts on bulk quantities of Jossey-Bass books are available
to corporations, professional associations, and other organizations. For
details and discount information, contact the special sales department at
Jossey-Bass Inc., Publishers. (415) 433-1740; Fax (415) 433-0499.

For sales outside the United States, please contact your local Paramount
Publishing International Office.

Library of Congress Cataloging-in-Publication Data

Hupp, Toni, date.
  Designing work groups, jobs, and work flow / Toni Hupp, with Craig
Polak and Odin Westgaard.
      p.   cm.—(From training to performance in the twenty-first
  century. Set 2, Redesigning work processes)
  Includes bibliographical references and index.
  ISBN 0-7879-0063-X
  1. Work groups. 2. Work design. 3. Job analysis. I. Polak, Craig, date. II.
Westgaard, Odin. III. Title. IV. Series.
HD66.H86   1995
658.4'02—dc20   94-37091

PB Printing 10 9 8 7 6 5 4 3 2 1   FIRST EDITION

**THE JOSSEY-BASS
MANAGEMENT SERIES**

CONTENTS

From Training to Performance in the Twenty-First Century: Introduction to the Book Series

For most trainers and instructional developers, the following request from a client sounds familiar: "I have a problem. Give me some training to solve it." We are taught to think that training is the answer to most human performance problems. But those of us who are veterans in the field have learned from our own experience and from others' research and theories that most of the problems our clients bring us are *not* best solved by training, or require some other solution in addition to training. What do we do in the face of this contradictory evidence?

We change our view of the world, our paradigm for thinking about how to solve our customers' problems. We look at practitioners in other fields and see how they recommend solving problems, and we try to incorporate their ideas and interventions into our own "bag of tricks."

We have heard and read about a wide array of such interventions: human-computer interface and workplace design; work process reengineering and sociotechnical systems; job aids, expert systems, and performance support systems; motivation, incentive, and feedback systems; organizational design, cultural change, and change management; measurement of results to demonstrate bottom-line savings. How do all these interventions fit together? Is there a field that incorporates and relates them? Yes. It is called Human Performance Technology (HPT).

What is human performance technology?

What makes HPT different from training, management consulting, and other practices aimed at improving the performance of people and organizations? According to Foshay and Moller (1992, p. 702), HPT is unique because it is "an applied field, not a discipline. it is structured primarily by the real world problem of human performance (in the workplace). It draws from any discipline that has prescriptive power in solving any human performance problem." Stolovitch and Keeps (1992, p. 7) have incorporated a variety of definitions of the field into their descriptions of HPT's unique approach to synthesizing ideas borrowed from other disciplines:

> *HPT, therefore, is an engineering approach to attaining desired accomplishments from human performers. HP technologists are those who adopt a systems view of performance gaps, systematically analyze both gap and system, and design cost-effective and efficient interventions that are based on analysis data, scientific knowledge, and documented precedents, in order to close the gap in the most desirable manner.*

Rummler and Brache (1992, p. 34) explain that the view HP technologists have of "what is going on . . . in organizations" is "fundamentally different" from views held by practitioners in other disciplines. HP technologists conceptualize "what is going on" by looking at and assessing three levels of variables that affect individual and organizational performance: the organization level, the work process level, and the job/worker level.

An HP technologist looks first at the total organization and at such variables as strategy and goals, structure, measurements, and management (see Figure P.1). Next, an HP technologist looks at work processes carried out across functions within the organization and analyzes the goals, design, measurement, and management of those processes to determine their effectiveness (see Figure P.2). Finally, an HP technologist looks at the job and the performer, focusing on five variables (Rummler and Brache, 1992, pp. 35–41):

1. *The performer.* Does the person have the physical, mental, and emotional ability as well as the skills and knowledge needed to perform?

2. *Inputs to the performer.* Are the available job procedures and work flow, information, money, tools, and the work environment adequate to support the desired performance?

3 *Outputs of the performer.* Do performance specifications for the outputs exist, and is the performer aware of them?

4. *Consequences of the performer's actions.* Are consequences designed to support the performance and delivered in a timely manner?

5. *Feedback the performer receives about the performance.* Does the performer receive feedback, and if so, is it relevant, timely, accurate, and specific?

Figure P.3 illustrates the relationship between these principles.

Figure P.1. The Organization View of Work.

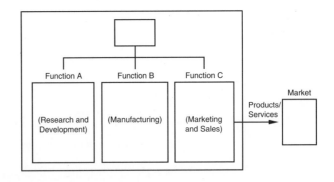

Source: Rummler and Brache, 1992, p. 35.

Figure P.2. The Cross-Functional View of Work Process.

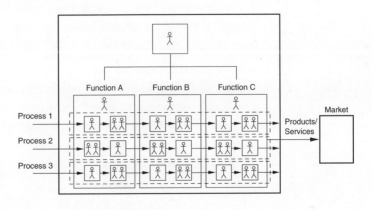

Source: Rummler and Brache, 1992, p. 37

Figure P.3. The Job/Performer View of Work.

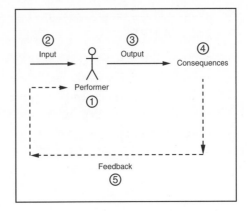

Source: Rummler and Brache, 1992, p. 38.

Purpose of the series

Once we have changed our worldview and accepted the notion of HPT interventions into our paradigm of how to approach the resolution of clients' problems, we would really like to try to implement some of them. But how?

1. Instruction is not the answer to every challenge in the workplace.

2. There are a wide array of interventions that can be used to enhance performance. . .

3. The HP technologist cannot be expected to be an expert in every intervention . . . [Rossett, 1992, p. 98].

As Rossett points out, it is not feasible for us to be experts in all these interventions. First, because the fields from which the interventions come are so diverse and constantly changing, it is virtually impossible for any of us to learn everything about and keep current in all fields. Second, there are very few resources out there to help us design and implement performance-enhancing interventions. Most books on the subject focus on what the interventions are and why they are important, but contain precious few specific guidelines, procedures, or rules for how to actually carry out the interventions.

So, as practitioners we face several gaps: between our grounding in the "training" field and the recognition that we need to expand our worldview to include other performance-enhancing interventions; between our desire to learn about the other interventions and the difficulty of keeping current in all the fields from which they derive; and between the desire to try performance-enhancing interventions and the lack of specific, practical guidance on how to do so.

The series "From Training to Performance in the Twenty-First Century" tries to bridge these gaps. First, the series is based on two assumptions: (1) that training/instructional design/HPT practitioners are, for the most part, currently limited to implementing training interventions in the workplace, and (2) that most practitioners recognize the need to broaden their worldview and range of interventions to embrace the approach described above. The series is designed to serve as a bridge from training to other areas of HPT.

Second, the series is a *translation/how-to-do-it* series that tracks down and summarizes the knowledge base of the fields from which the performance-enhancing interventions are derived and focuses on specific, practical, *how-to* techniques for implementing performance-enhancing interventions in real job situations.

Organization of the series

To accomplish our purposes, we have organized the series into manageable chunks called Sets, each comprising two to five books that address a related set of performance-enhancing interventions. Each book covers one performance-enhancing intervention completely.

To implement the translation/how-to-do-it approach, maintain consistency across the series, and make the procedures as easy as possible to learn and use, each book makes extensive use of procedure and decision tables, forms, examples (both successful and unsuccessful), and case studies. Each book begins with a brief synthesis of the theoretical foundations of the intervention, acknowledging different points of view where they exist. This introductory material is followed by chapters containing a wide variety of procedures that show how to implement each intervention step by step. Many job aids and forms are provided. The book presents one or more real-world case studies showing the entire intervention in practice, complete with filled-out forms. It also provides a resource section that contains blank forms for reproduction. Finally, an extensive bibliography covers almost all the current thinking about the intervention.

Audience

The "From Training to Performance" series is designed for three audiences. The primary audience is trainers, training managers, and novice HPT practitioners, who will use the books as an on-the-job reference and work tool as they move from applying training solutions to using performance improvement interventions. The second audience is longtime instructional design and HPT practitioners, who will use the books for continuing education in performance improvement interventions that have evolved since they joined the filed. The third audience is graduate students in training, instructional design, performance technology, organizational development, human resource development, and management, who will use the books to learn HPT techniques.

Each audience will use the series slightly differently. Trainers and training managers might want to begin with the case studies to see how the intervention really works, then go to the procedures and forms to try out the interventions. Graduate students will almost certainly begin with the theoretical material and integrate it into their schema of HPT before moving on to apply the procedures and forms to real-world or simulated performance problems. Veteran HPT practitioners might use either of the approaches, jumping back and forth between the procedures, case study and theory, or focusing on the design and usability of the procedures and forms that are of particular professional interest to them.

It is the fervent hope of the National Society for Performance and Instruction (NSPI) that readers will use the books in this series as a continuing source of self-development, training for others, and, most important, on-the-job reference tools, to provide clients with the most cost-effective and efficient interventions for solving their business problems.

Acknowledgments

This series would not exist without the help and support of the following people, who helped create and nurture it: the late Paul Tremper, NSPI's executive director from 1985 to 1993, who provided vision and emotional support for the series and expert handling of the seemingly infinite details associated with the series at NSPI; Maurice Coleman, vice president of research and development at NSPI in 1991, and the 1991 publications committee, whose idea it was to create the series: Esther Powers (1991 NSPI president), Roger Addison (1992 NSPI president), William Coscarelli (1992 vice president of publications), and Kathleen Whiteside (1993 NSPI president), who led their boards of directors in providing emotional and financial support for the series from the beginning to the present; the topic editors and authors of the series, who through vision, intelligence, and perseverance transformed the idea of the series into the book you are now reading; Sarah Polster, editor of the management series at Jossey-Bass, who taught us what the business of publishing was all about, helped formulate the final look, feel, and chapter structure, negotiated the sometimes rough waters between our dreams about the series and what could actually be done, and coordinated the learning everyone at both NSPI and Jossey-Bass did about working together and producing a state-of-the-art series using state-of-the-art technology; Barbara Hill at Jossey-Bass, who coordinated all the deadlines, manuscripts, authors, reviews, and many other things we're glad not to have known about; Judith A. Hale, President, Hale Associates, who saw the value of the series and my involvement in it and continually and generously supported my efforts.

Dedication

This series is dedicated to a forgotten leader in the HPT field and in NSPI: the 1963 "Man of the Year in Programming," whose ideas formed the early basis for HPT's processes and interventions; a visionary who challenged the status quo, always with logic, reason, and passion; a teacher, guide, and friend who pushed his students to exemplary performance, encouraged them also to challenge the status quo, assisted them in their journey, and then rewarded their successes lavishly. The series is dedicated to the late James D. Finn, with respect and thanks for all he gave to me personally as my mentor, to those (too numerous to mention) who knew and worked with him, and to the field and profession of Human Performance Technology.

Chicago, Illinois
January 1994

Kenneth H. Silber
Series Editor

Redesigning Work Processes: About This Group of Books

What is the purpose of these books?

- "Management wants us to get the work out faster. Well, it won't get any faster as long as the process is hurry up, wait, and then do it again."

- "Management wants Marketing and Engineering to work together more efficiently. Well, they can't be efficient if they keep doing each other's work instead of what needs to be done."

- "Don't those instructional designers know something about finding out what people really do? Maybe they can help us analyze processes too."

- "Don't trainers know how to facilitate groups? Why don't we put one of them on the team charged to redesign our process?"

These statements reflect organizations' increasing awareness that processes affect productivity, and their growing expectation that trainers can contribute valuable skills to the process redesign.

The term *process* is used to represent all the activities that must happen to produce a product or offer a service. A process is how things get done, whether by people, machines, or both. Processes are not always designed. They may be a hodge-podge of activities that evolved over time in response to immediate pressures and personal work preferences. How work gets done may reflect an organization's needs rather than its customer's needs. A process is designed when there is a purposeful examination of what must happen and how to best do what is required to satisfy customer needs.

The two books in this group will prepare the reader to purposefully examine processes and identify what is needed to make those processes more efficient and effective. Both books provide a model that trainers and instructional technologists may use to leverage their already strong job and task analysis, facilitation, and project management skills.

How do these books fit in the series?

The two books in this group are a subset of the series From Training to Performance in the Twenty-First Century. They focus on how to describe, analyze, and redesign processes. They give readers the procedures and guidelines they need to be knowledgeable participants on process redesign teams.

Designing Work Groups, Jobs, and Work Flow, by Toni Hupp (with Craig Polak and Odin Westgaard), provides a basic understanding of how to describe, analyze, and redesign processes used by intact work groups within a specific function (see Figure P.4). The book will give readers a better understanding of how to identify all the activities a work group engages in. It includes procedures for capturing who does what and why, when, how, and toward what outcome they do it. It also provides procedures and guidelines for improving processes.

Figure P.4.

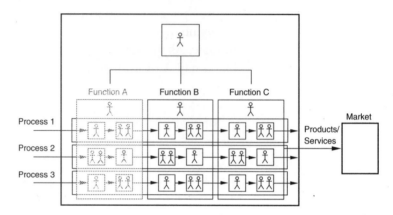

Designing Cross-Functional Business Processes, by Bernard Johann, focuses on how to identify, describe, analyze, and redesign processes that bridge traditional functional or departmental lines (see Figure P.5).

It, too, includes procedures for documenting what actually happens. It also discusses specific steps readers can follow to make incremental improvements and major redesign changes in existing processes.

Figure P.5.

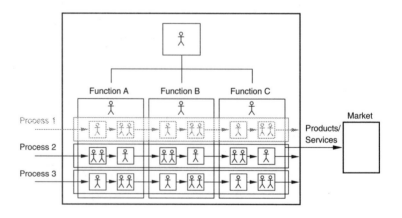

Western Springs, Illinois
January 1995

Judith A. Hale
Topic Editor

Preface

When competition "raises the bar," and "the way things have always been done" won't cut it anymore, people often jump to the conclusion that someone needs fixing. Training practitioners often go along with this leap in logic. As the saying goes, if all you have is a hammer, everything looks like a nail. Unfortunately, you rarely change "the way things have always been done" in an organization simply by retraining its people. When an organization's structure and work flow prevent it from reaching its goals, training alone won't solve the problem.

This pair of books explains how to design systems to fit their environments' demands and stakeholders' needs. Bernard Johann's book, *Designing Cross-Functional Business Processes,* describes how to design large-scale, multifunctional processes involving more than one work group. This book explains how to design a single work group's processes, composition, and individual jobs. Both books examine work processes — that is, how work gets done. The difference is that Johann focuses on how to design a big process, such as Research and Development or Manufacturing, that cuts across many work groups. This book focuses on how to design a smaller process, the process a single work group uses to create its product or service. You'll find that you use many of the same principles and tools to design a smaller, single-purpose process. This book shows you design at a "grass-roots" level. It shows you how to design day-to-day work flows, group structures, and job responsibilities to maximize local ownership and responsiveness.

Background of the book

In the months since work on this book began, reengineering and process redesign have become among the hottest topics in the business press. At the same time, colleagues close to the redesign/reengineering action note the increasing frequency with which they're asked to mop up after botched redesign/reengineering projects. These failed efforts typically amount to glorified automation, downsizing, or redrawing of political turf. While these perennial purges succeed in cutting head counts (albeit temporarily), they fail to provoke a fundamental rethinking of the targeted unit's purpose, process, and people. They leave a dispirited work force, exhausted and risk-averse managers, and a confused and inwardly focused organizational culture—hardly the stuff from which world-class competition is made.

This situation leads to the notion that something must be missing in the hundreds of books and articles on the subject. The first missing or unstated element is an acknowledgment of the redo mentality prevalent in today's workplace. This is the type of thinking that occurs when people perform design, redesign, or reengineering with the belief that if it doesn't work, they or someone else can *re*design or *re*engineer over and over until they get it right. This is not exactly the kind of thinking that should be found in an organization that seriously wants to improve the quality of its operations. This book tackles that issue by providing the tools and techniques to do design or redesign right . . . the first time.

The next missing piece in those books and articles turns out to be exactly those tools and techniques needed to actually *do* work group and job design. Theories and success stories have their place. But if the tools and techniques are missing, they leave people to their own devices to make up their own. This book confronts that dilemma by giving you the tools and step-by-step techniques you need to perform design or redesign efforts competently and completely.

Audience

This book can help managers, performance technologists, instructional designers, and work teams to think through the ecology as well as the economy of their work. It challenges readers to examine how well their business units' purposes align with their customers' needs. It challenges doers to examine how well their technical process supports quality, responsiveness, and ownership of their products and services. It challenges all to come up with structures and systems that maximize initiative, ownership, and flexibility. In short, it explains how to create jobs and work groups that can sustain high levels of performance through leaner processes and enhanced job ownership.

Overview of the contents

The heart of this book focuses on the critical steps of any design effort, be it instructional or process design. Those steps are analysis and design. With strong analysis and design work, implementation almost always comes easily. Without it, you are almost certain to face failure.

However, the book does speak to your needs before and after analysis and design. Those needs include scoping the design and then implementing it. The procedures contained in these chapters will hopefully provide insight into how those activities will play out in a work-group or job design effort.

Designing Work Groups, Jobs, and Work Flow is organized into four sections. Section One describes how to decide on the model that's right for your work group's needs, technology, and environment. It explains the concepts and principles you need to design a better local system (work flow, work group, and jobs).

Section Two describes how to first initiate and scope a work-group or job design project. Analyzing the chosen process is next, followed by the design phase. Section Two ends with implementing the new process, which should flow smoothly if you've given careful attention to analysis and design.

Section Three provides a case study of the entire process in action.

Section Four provides tools and job aids to guide your own design efforts.

Acknowledgments

The ideas in this book are not new. This book merely applies the ideas of intellectual forefathers and mothers to the grass-roots level. For the vision of self-designing systems I thank Susan Albers Mohrman, Thomas Cummings, David Hanna, William Lytle, Edward Lawler, and Gareth Morgan. For the vision of whole, unfragmented processes managed for continuous improvement I thank authors Michael Hammer and James Champy, James Harrington, Lawrence Miller, William Pasmore, Geary Rummler and Alan Brache, and George Robson. For the vision of whole, meaningful, involving work I thank authors Richard Hackman and Greg Oldham, Edward Lawler, Robert Tomasko, and my colleague Peter Sorenson. For the vision of empowering governance structures I thank authors Peter Block and Edward Lawler and colleagues Steve Treacy and Nan Voss. For job design ideas I thank Peter Sorenson. For examples and case studies I thank Odin Westgaard.

For encouragement of mind, heart, and spirit I thank my husband and life-long best friend, Bob Hupp.

Warrenville, Illinois   Toni Hupp
January 1995

The Authors

Toni Hupp is vice president of training and organization development for Bank of America. She consults with clients on organizational and job design, team building, process mapping and improvement, and creating peformance management systems to support a more self-directed work environment. She also manages management development/professional development staff.

In the past she has managed a successful consulting business in performance technology and has taught consulting skills, instructional design, and performance technology in both higher education (Governors State University) and industry (Arthur Andersen, Applied Learning International, Covia Partnership).

Hupp earned her M.S. Ed. (1987) in instructional technology at Southern Illinois University and her B.S. degree (1973) at Southern Illinois University. She has received training in performance engineering and process redesign from performance technology "founding fathers" Tom Gilbert, Joe Harless, and Geary Rummler. She is currently doing graduate studies in management and organizational behavior at Illinois Benedictine College.

Hupp has an active service record with the National Society of Performance and Instruction (NSPI), having chaired various committees at both the national and local levels (Chicago chapter). She is a recipient of NSPI's Special Service Award (1993) and was honored as the Chicago chapter's Member of the Year (1986).

Craig Polak is a consultant to management, skilled in instructional design, education, communication, and competency assessment. In 1989 he joined Hale Associates, a leader in providing innovative and practical approaches to performance improvement. He has since assisted in many intervention activities, including development of leadership communication courses; certification program development for several audiences, including the training profession; and design of skills enhancement programs.

Polak's varied experiences include employment and volunteer roles in management, government, journalism, research, writing, and education. Craig is schooled in political science, which has given him the opportunity to effectively serve as a civic volunteer.

Polak is a member of the National Society for Performance and Instruction (NSPI) and its Chicago chapter. He also serves as Hale Associates' representative to the National Organization for Competency Assurance (NOCA).

He earned his M.S. Ed. (1989) in instructional design at Purdue University and his B.A. (1978) in political science, also at Purdue. He also successfully completed Indiana's Secondary Education Teacher Certification Program (1987) at Purdue.

Odin Westgaard is a human systems interventionist with Hale Associates, a top-rated management consultant company serving the Chicago area. He earned his B.A. (1962) in mathematics at Western State College of Colorado and both his M.A. (1968) in school administration and Statistics and his Ed.D. degree (1970) in curriculum development at the University of Northern Colorado. Before joining Hale, Westgaard worked as a specialist in training for industry, and before that as a professor of education.

Westgaard has written extensively for professional journals on measurement and evaluation, the training process, and peripheral arenas. He has written or coauthored four books, *Instructional Design Competencies, The Standards* (1981); *The Competent Manager's Handbook for Measuring Unit Productivity* (1985); *The Competent Manager's Handbook for Selecting and Evaluating Training* (1987); and *Good Fair Tests* (1993). He edited the CNSPI journal, *Chicago P & I,* and was associate editor of the *P & I Journal.* He is a regular contributor to *Performance and Instruction Quarterly,* for which he writes a column on historical figures in the profession called *Allow Me to Introduce . . .* He is currently a member of the publications board for the Chicago chapter of ASTD and the Chicago chapter of NSPI.

Westgaard has served as chapter president for PDK and NSPI. He was nominated for NSPI Member of the Year, and has served that organization as a committee chair (measurement and evaluation track) and committee member (ethics and others). He was one of the original members of the board for the International Board of Standards for Training, Performance, and Instruction (IBSTPI) and served in that capacity for eight years. He's currently part of IBSTPI's effort to develop certification for professionals and organizations in the field.

Series Editor

Kenneth H. Silber, an associate at Hale Associates, has been contributing to the performance technology and instructional design fields since their beginnings thirty years ago. He has worked in corporate, non-profit, academic, and consulting settings internationally, designing and implementing performance improvement interventions. Silber's interventions have assisted numerous management, sales, and technical professionals with the deployment of new systems, new work processes, and new quality processes, all supported by business rationales that justify the interventions to upper management.

Silber has worked with clients to align strategic plans and product/service mixes with corporate directions and customer requirements; to reengineer work processes to reduce cycle time and costs while improving customer responsiveness; to do needs assessments and eliminate or redirect ineffective and inappropriate training; to design solutions to improve performance through environmental, technological, job-aid, work process, works standards development and documentation, certification, and feedback/motivation interventions. Before coming to Hale, Silber worked at Governors State University, AT&T, ASI/DELTAK/ALI, and Amoco. Both as a professor and a consultant, Silber has trained over one thousand workers to do process reengineering, peformance improvement, needs assessment, and instructional design.

Silber is a nationally recognized and published author and professional leader. He has coauthored three books, including the International Board of Standards for Training, Performance & Instruction's (IBSTPI) *Instructional Design Competencies: The Standards.* A fourth book, *Training That Works: How to Train Anybody to Do Anything,* is currently in press. Silber started and edited the *Journal of Instructional Development,* wrote chapters for the American Society for Training and Development's (ASTD) *Training and Development Handbook* and NSPI's *Handbook of Human Performance Technology,* and has published over fifty other articles and monographs. A former member of the Executive Committee of the Association for Educational Communications and Technology (AECT) and of IBSTPI, he has also served as past president of the Chicago Chapter of NSPI.

Silber holds a Ph.D. in instructional technology from the University of Southern California (1969) and a B.A. from the University of Rochester (1965).

Topic Editor

Judith A. Hale has been a consultant to business for over twenty years. The founder of Hale Associates, she has worked with companies to develop and improve work processes in manufacturing, customer service, assessment, and people development. Her work is recognized as innovative and practical. Her firm has developed new approaches to strategic planning, competence assessment, process design, leadership development, team building, and certification.

Hale has developed a process that training functions can use to evaluate how well they assess customer needs, provide leadership on learning and performance improvement issues, establish measures, qualify instructors, and design, develop, and deliver instructional programs. The process complements those used in ISO 9000 certifications and the Baldrige Award. It will be used by the International Board of Standards to certify training departments, instructors, instructional designers, and instructional products. Her book *How to Apply the Quality Principles to Training,* currently in press, includes procedures to evaluate how well training's processes follow the standards espoused by ISO and Baldrige.

Hale is a member of the American Society for Training and Development (ASTD) and the National Society of Performance and Instruction (NSPI). She was president of the International Board of Standards for Training, Performance, and Instruction (IBSTPI); the Chicago chapter of the Industrial Relations Research Association (IRRA); and the Chicago chapter of the National Society of Performance and Instruction (CNSPI). She was a commercial arbitrator with the American Arbitration Association and an assistant professor of communications for six years. The Insurance School of Chicago acknowledged her fourteen years of excellence to management education with its "Outstanding Educator" award in 1986. NSPI recognized her contributions to the profession with its "Outstanding Member of the Year" award in 1987.

Hale holds a Ph.D. in instructional technology from Purdue University (1991), an M.A. in communications from Miami University (1965), and a B.A. in communications from Ohio State University (1963).

HOW WORK GROUP DESIGN AFFECTS PEOPLE, PRODUCTS, AND SERVICES

Overview

What is this section about?

Section One will show how current work systems (work processes, groups, and jobs) become out-of-date and out of sync with their environments. When they do, they can break and collapse. This section confronts that issue by showing you

- Why current systems often fail
- How these failures end up at your doorstep
- Why training alone won't fix these failures
- What *will* fix system failures
- What principles to use to design a healthier system
- What components to examine when looking at a work group's local system
- What results healthier systems typically produce

Section One also describes how to decide on an organizational model that's right for your work group's needs, technology, and environment. It explains the concepts and principles you need to know to design a better local system (work flow, work group, and jobs).

How is this section organized?

CHAPTER 1

What Makes a Work Group or Department Effective?

Why Should I Read This Book?

The need to design processes, work groups, and jobs

Today our organizations face accelerating demands. These demands call for

- Increasingly specialized products and services to address ever more narrowly defined market niches
- Faster time-to-market
- Better quality
- More responsive service

And all these demands must be met with fewer resources! It's no wonder they overload existing capacities.

When organizations need to boost their capacity, they often turn to approaches such as training, reorganization, and even cutting back product lines. All these approaches treat a *single slice* of how an organization works. They don't align the *whole system* so that all its pieces pull in the same direction. As Geary Rummler and Alan Brache warn (1990), "Pulling any lever in the system will have an effect on other parts of the system. You can't just reorganize, or just train, or just automate, as if you were merely adding some spice to the stew. Each of these actions changes the recipe" (p. 13).

Not only have past approaches been piecemeal, they have fragmented work and obstructed the "big picture." Ever since industrialization began, organizations have attempted to improve their capacity by breaking large efforts into their simplest, most narrowly defined tasks and closely managing each of the tasks. However, as a large effort becomes more and more complex, the work of each contributor becomes more and more fragmented. In addition, although managers closely manage work *within* each narrowly defined task, seldom do they manage the overall work flow *across* tasks and functions. The more fragmented the work becomes, the greater the need for coordination.

The business cost of fragmentation

Our old approach of breaking work down into increasingly specialized tasks can turn into a coordination nightmare that single-handedly defeats the purpose of faster time-to-market, better quality, and more responsive service. In *Reengineering the Corporation,* Hammer and Champy (1993) discuss how this happens:

> *Today, fragmented organizations display appalling diseconomies of scale, quite the opposite of what Adam Smith envisioned. The diseconomies of scale show up* not *in direct labor, but in overhead. If, for instance, an organization does 100 units of work an hour, and each of its workers can do 10 units an hour, the company would need 11 people: 10 workers and 1 supervisor. But if demand for the company's output grew tenfold to 1,000 units of work per hour, the company wouldn't need just 10 times the number of workers plus one manager for each 10 new workers. It would need something like 196 people: 100 workers, 10 supervisors, 1 manager, 3 assistant managers, 18 people in human resources, 19 people in long-range planning, 22 in audit and control, and 23 in facilitation and expediting.*

> *This diseconomy of scale is not just bureaucratic proliferation and empire-building. Rather, it is a consequence of what we call the Humpty Dumpty School of Organizational Management. Companies take a natural process, such as order fulfillment, and break it into lots of little pieces — the individual tasks that people in the functional departments do. Then, the company has to hire all the king's horses and all the king's men to paste the fragmented work back together again. These king's horses and king's men have titles such as auditor, expediter, controller, liaison, supervisor, manager, and vice president. They are simply the glue that holds together the people who do the* real *work — the credit checkers, the inventory pickers, the package shippers. In many companies, direct labor costs may be down, but overhead costs are up — way up. Most companies today, in other words, are paying more for the glue than for the real work — a recipe for trouble (pp. 29–30).*

This fragmentation of work exacts a toll, not only on the business as a whole, but on the individual worker as well.

The human cost of fragmentation

Fragmentation of work can force workers to spend more than half their waking hours doing narrowly defined tasks with little idea of how these tasks add to the end product or service. Because the worker does not see the final result, he or she is cut off from intrinsic feedback. Fragmentation also typically separates thinking (planning and controlling) from doing; thinking is reserved for management. It provides little autonomy and little opportunity to develop skills beyond a narrow range of tasks. Studs Terkel (1974) evokes the impact that fragmented work can have on the human spirit in his introduction to *Working*:

> *For the many, there is a hardly concealed discontent. The blue-collar blues is no more bitterly sung than the white-collar moan. "I'm a machine," says the spot-welder. "I'm caged," says the bank teller, and echoes the hotel clerk. "I'm a mule," says the steel-worker. "A monkey can do what I do," says the receptionist. "I'm less than a farm implement," says the migrant worker. Blue collar and white call upon the identical phrase: "I'm a robot" (p. xiv).*

In the early days of industrialization, fragmentation of work grew out of the need to employ cheap, minimally skilled labor and foreign workers in mass production. To minimize the need for advanced skills and language fluency, industrial engineers — led by Frederick Winslow Taylor — broke down, simplified, and specialized tasks. Taylor called this approach "scientific management," and it's best exemplified in traditional assembly line work. Today, fragmentation and specialization continue, in spite of an increasingly educated work force. In *Work Redesign*, Hackman and Oldham (1980) point out the impact this has on the work force:

> *In sum, even as work organizations have continued to get bigger, more mechanistic, more controlling of individual behavior, and more task-specialized, the people who work in those organizations have become more highly educated, more desirous of "intrinsic" work satisfactions, and perhaps less willing to accept routine and monotonous work as their legitimate lot in life. . . . We may now have arrived at a point where the way most organizations function is in severe conflict with the talents and aspirations of the people who work in them. Such conflict manifests itself in increased alienation from work and in decreased organizational effectiveness, as evidenced in sagging attendance and productivity figures (p. 8).*

So what's the overall problem?

Fragmented processes and oversimplified work can be symptoms of a misaligned system. The systems that worked with a largely unskilled labor force in a less competitive economy no longer work with today's more educated labor force and highly competitive global economy. Change creates problems of fit. When an organization's demands, resources, or constraints change but its internal design remains the same, it will suffer problems of fit. When a work group changes one aspect of its internal design (for instance, to take advantage of new technology) but fails to adapt other aspects of its internal design accordingly, it will suffer problems of fit.

However, in many organizations, it's misleading to talk about "design." In fact, it's likely that no one consciously designed the current system; it "just kinda happened." No one designed reward systems to punish performance. No one designed the work process to pit one group of contributors against another. No one designed a work process in which heroes and heroines succeed more in spite of a convoluted work flow than because of it. These things happened in the absence of design.

When you consciously design a system, you design mutually reinforcing parts that can anticipate needs and adapt to changes. For the purposes of this book, you can think of a system in three parts:

1. **The environment** and the demands and goals that it triggers
2. **The technical process** — in other words, how things get done
3. **The human structure and support systems** — in other words, how people are organized, how work gets distributed, and what gets rewarded

Environmental changes. Environmental changes that often drive the need for design include

- Increased competition
- Higher customer expectations
- Economic turbulence
- Access to new markets

Technical process. Conditions that often indicate a need for a better technical process include demands for

- Shorter cycle-times
- Less in-process inventory
- Less waste or downtime
- Integration of new technology

Human structure and support systems. Conditions that often indicate a need for a better human structure and support system include demands for

- More flexible deployment of the organization's labor force
- More responsiveness, innovation, and ownership from production and front-line employees
- More satisfying work

When you change any of these three areas, the others will change in response. They may change by design or by default, but they *will* change. To make all parts mutually reinforcing, you need to change them by design.

What this problem means to you

When the system's parts are working at cross-purposes, it can be so transparent that employees each assume someone else is to blame. It simply never occurs to them to suspect a bad system. They conclude that *others* lack skill, motivation, or character. They figure that training departments fix people, so they bring their problems to your doorstep.

This finger-pointing can begin at any level. Upper management wonders why it takes twice as long for the organization to bring a new product to market as their competitors take. They decide that their employees need better technical skills, or that management needs to eliminate unpredictable human delays through automation. In the latter case, they ask you to train people to work with the automated system.

But when you investigate this alleged performance deficiency you hear from the workers that their groups have met their numbers. They say the other groups seem more interested in ducking responsibility and fixing blame than fixing problems. They suggest that you train the other groups to be better "team players."

Meanwhile, the other groups' supervisors maintain that their priorities seem to be constantly changing. They speculate that senior managers seem incapable of making up their minds; they will establish a new direction and then, at just about the time supervisors get everyone headed in the new direction, they change course. The supervisors suggest that you train senior management in "leadership skills."

No one succeeds in such a system. As Rummler and Brache (1990) warn, "If you pit a good performer against a bad system, the system will win almost every time. We spend too much of our time 'fixing' people who are *not* broken, and not enough time fixing organization systems that are broken" (p. 13).

Moving from training to performance

When faced with the situations described above, many training practitioners focus on finding out whether employees know how to do their jobs. After identifying skill deficits, they design training or job aids to improve those skills. But if they're working with a misaligned system, the result could be a small improvement that still can't match the competition. If the problem is a bad work process, such as one requiring multiple sign-offs at key decision points, the answer is *not* simply to teach employees to do their jobs better. The answer is to design a new work process and a corresponding authority structure to support it.

This requires a larger perspective than your average trainer's. It requires a human performance technologist's perspective. A trainer typically focuses on how to improve *individual* performance. A human performance technologist focuses on how to improve *systemwide* performance. Analysis examines things such as

- The environment's demands and customer requirements. (How fast must a new product get to market? What do customers expect?)

- The technical process. (How much of the total time is spent on value-adding tasks? How can the process be streamlined?)

- The human structure and systems, including allocation of authority and responsibility. (Does decision-making authority rest with those who have the best information with which to make the decision?)

These questions examine the whole system, not just the contributions of individual players. In defining human performance technology, Stolovich and Keeps (1992) say, "Human performance technologists take a systemic (total system) approach to performance analysis and change, as opposed to making piecemeal interventions" (p. 4).

In addition, to design congruent work processes, groups, and jobs, human performance technologists apply principles of process improvement, organizational theory, sociotechnical systems design, and job design. These practices are explained below:

- *Process improvement* ensures that the work flow is streamlined and unfragmented.

- *Organizational theory* ensures that a work group's form fits its function.

- *Sociotechnical systems design* ensures that the newly designed system simultaneously improves both business results and the quality of work life. This requires that you involve employees in designing the systems to which they contribute.

- *Job design* ensures that jobs build employee ownership and initiative.

Why design processes, groups, and jobs?

When you design processes, groups, and jobs, you can get

- **Better coordination and information flow.** When you organize work around whole products or services, people who need to cooperate with each other are on the same team, focused on a common goal. (In the past, work has typically been organized around functions, putting people who need to cooperate with each other on different work groups pursuing function-specific goals.)

- **Reduced costs and cycle times.** When you streamline work flow, you remove or minimize non–value adding steps. This reduces costs, cycle times, and opportunities for error. In addition, when mature work teams plan and monitor their own work, you need fewer managers. The managers who remain can focus on integrating efforts across teams and developing business strategy.

- **Improved responsiveness to customers.** When you organize work around products, services, or customer groups, employees get greater access to customers, become better at anticipating customer needs, and provide better-informed, more responsive customer service.

- **More innovation.** When you provide employees with the opportunity and responsibility to improve their products, services, and processes, you shorten the distance between ideas and their implementation.

- **More value added through people.** When employees produce whole products or services, not isolated fragments, they have more ownership in their job. Also, jobs that integrate thinking with doing result in greater job satisfaction. Finally, when managers focus on integrating instead of supervising, they concentrate on getting people to work together across boundaries, not second-guessing individual efforts. This focuses them on adding value, not on reworking their subordinates' work.

- **More flexibility.** When an organization deploys a broadly skilled work force it gets more flexibility than when it deploys a narrowly skilled one.

How to design processes, work groups, and jobs

To design a process, lead your clients in anticipating customer needs and choosing the most appropriate method to produce customer-satisfying products and services. Next, facilitate the streamlining and error-proofing of that method's work flow. Finally, help design an information lifeline that provides doers with the information they need to anticipate needs, evaluate operations, and troubleshoot.

To design a work group, help your clients find out who participates in their process. To ensure an unfragmented work flow, organize these people together on the same team. Next, help your clients design a structure that gives people the authority to respond to needs and problems. Finally, help your clients select coordination mechanisms to manage their boundaries with other work groups so that work flows across boundaries without encountering barriers, bottlenecks, blind spots, or "black holes."

To design jobs, help your clients group tasks into jobs that produce whole products or services. Make sure these jobs unite thinking tasks, such as planning, with doing tasks, such as assembling. Also integrate support tasks, such as checking and troubleshooting, with core production or delivery tasks. Finally, help your clients to establish direct contacts between jobholders and their customers, so that each jobholder gets firsthand feedback from customers.

This book focuses on organizational design at a "grass-roots" level. However, organizational design at any level involves

- Identifying which system you want to focus on.

- Identifying the environmental demands on that system and the goals it's expected to accomplish

- Determining how well its technical processes and corresponding human structures and systems support it in reaching its goals

- Modifying the technical processes and corresponding human structures and systems to make them more successful at accomplishing what they're supposed to accomplish

From this definition you can see that organizational design does *not* mean doing any of the following things *in isolation:*

- Restructuring

- Down-sizing or right-sizing

- Pruning the product or service line

- Merging, acquiring, or divesting

- Redrawing job boundaries or redefining jobs

- Installing new appraisal and compensation systems

Each of these interventions only focuses on a slice of the systemwide performance; organizational design focuses on an entire system. It may focus on a microsystem, such as a work group, or on a macrosystem, such as an entire business, yet it always focuses on an entire system.

What do well-designed work processes look like?

A work process determines how work gets done. It consists of tasks, which can be further broken down into steps and/or decisions. A well-designed work process is streamlined and unfragmented. It is supported by an information flow that provides doers with an accurate picture of customer needs and process performance. A well-designed work process should

- Be organized around a whole product or service. (It should *not* be obstructed by organizational boundaries, gaps, stalls, redundancies, or other inefficiencies.)

- Produce a result that meets requirements efficiently, effectively, and consistently.

- Consist of as few steps as possible. (The more lengthy and complex the process, the greater the chance that something will go wrong, and the longer the cycle time.)

- Include as few non–value added steps as possible and spend minimal time on any non–value added step. (A non–value added step is one that fails to produce a valuable change in the product or service.)

- Minimize midprocess handoffs. (An efficient work process involves as few people as possible.)

- Contain built-in checkpoints so that contributors can quickly detect and correct problems.

- Minimize second-party checking. (Contributors should be responsible for checking their own work. Use second-party inspection points only when there's a sufficient cost-benefit justification.)

- Minimize reconciliation. Aim to cut back on the number of related documents or contacts that must be reconciled (such as receipts, invoices, and purchase orders). The fewer times contributors must input information about a transaction, the less opportunity there is for error. Combine related documents or contacts.

- Identify a single point of customer contact. Construct information-source networks and provide computerized access to records so that the customer contact person can easily locate answers to customer questions.

- Tolerate as much environmental variability as possible.

- Make the most of both technical capacities and available human capacities.

The above guidelines are based on principles of process design (Hammer and Champy [1993], Harbour [1993], and Miller and Howard [1991]) and on principles of sociotechnical systems design (Pasmore [1988]).

What do well-designed work groups look like?

A work group is a group of people who share common goals, resources, outputs, and a common reporting relationship. A well-designed work group includes players with the depth and variety of skills necessary to create a whole product or service. Their roles should integrate thinking with doing, and support core production. The group's authority structure should provide employees with the autonomy and self-control they need to respond to the needs and problems nearest to their lines of action. A well-designed work group should

- Be organized around a process that creates a whole product or service (or at least a discrete, meaningful part of one).

- Have a start-to-finish view of what it takes to satisfy its customers. It should have the information and power necessary to do whatever it takes to meet customer requirements consistently.

- Have boundaries that do not present barriers to information flow, coordination, and shared ownership of the product or service.

- Be constrained by only those rules and task procedures that are critical to the process's success.

- Encompass all the skills necessary to produce its products or services. The group's collective skill set should include both the management skills needed to plan and control the process and the technical skills needed to execute and maintain the process.

- Consist of members who are each competent in multiple skills required by the group's work process, so that the work group can minimize handoffs and be flexible and adaptive.

What do well-designed jobs look like?

A job is all the tasks and responsibilities assigned to a single contributor. A well-designed job is organized around a meaningful product or service. It unites thinking with doing, and supports core production. It provides the jobholder direct contact with the customer. A well-designed job should

- Supply contributors with the information they need to take action, make decisions, or seize opportunities that their tasks present.

- Supply contributors with the information and resources they need to spot and correct mistakes at their point of origin.

- Provide variety by requiring the use of a range of different skills.

- Provide identity by creating a whole, meaningful unit of work.

- Provide significance by creating something that makes a difference

- Provide autonomy by allowing members to determine their methods, priorities, pacing, and so on.

- Provide intrinsic feedback about performance. *Intrinsic* feedback comes from the work itself, as well as its results.

The above work group and job design principles are based on principles of work design (Hackman and Oldham [1980], Tomasko [1993]) and on principles of sociotechnical systems design (Pasmore [1988]).

What Are the Results of Improving Processes, Work Groups, and Jobs?

When a work group designs a more organic system, it will have

- A grass-roots system that's self-regulating and more responsive to its business context

- A work process that's fast, focused, and flexible

- A work group with the collective expertise to plan, coordinate, control, and troubleshoot its own work

- Jobs that build contributors' ownership and commitment

Getting the "Big Picture"

The parts of the "big picture"

To change the way a system works, you need to know the parts that make up the system and how those parts work together. Without this framework, you can get lost in detail, miss important connections, and end up recommending a multitude of isolated tactics without developing any unifying strategy or purpose to focus your efforts.

The "big picture" that you will analyze and design is the system. As mentioned earlier, for the purposes of this book, you can think of a system in three parts:

1. **The environment** and the demands and goals that it triggers

2. **The technical process**—in other words, how things get done

3. **The human structure and support systems**—in other words, how people are organized, how work gets distributed, and what gets rewarded

In the sections that follow you will take a closer look at each of these parts.

1. The environment, demands, and goals

The environment shapes the work group's goals and provides the resources upon which it depends. A work group's environment presents both external and internal demands. The external demands include the expectations of regulators and suppliers and the market's appetite for the work group's products and/or services. Internal demands include competitive strategies and employee expectations. Employees can have the capacity and expectation for either challenging entrepreneurial work or routine, narrowly defined work.

Different environments demand different approaches to work group design:

A. *Environmental conditions that call for an organic, involvement-building design*: When the organization as a whole operates in a growing or dynamic market or its competitive strategy focuses on growing its market share, the work group needs a design that's organic—in other words, one that's flat, fast, and flexible, with relatively

- Unrestricted flows of information
- Dispersed planning and control
- Dispersed decision making, based on expertise
- Flexible operating procedures that provide only minimal critical specifications

Furthermore, when the labor force expects challenging and entrepreneurial work, job designs must build ownership and initiative.

B. *Environmental conditions that permit a mechanistic, control-oriented design*: When the organization as a whole operates in a stable or declining market, or is part of a highly regulated industry, its competitive strategy typically focuses on maintaining or exiting from its current market share. Under these conditions a work group can get by with a traditional mechanistic design — in other words, one that's hierarchical, bureaucratic, and fixed, with relatively

- Restricted flows of information
- Hierarchical, centralized planning and control
- Clear chains of command, with narrow spans of control
- Rigid and detailed standard operating procedures

Given the rate of change in today's business environment, mechanistic designs are becoming less and less appropriate. Consequently, this book will not show how to build a mechanistic design.

The above discussion is based on Lawler's (1992) description of decision factors and on literature on organizational growth stages by Brandt (1982), Churchill and Lewis (1983), Davidow and Uttal (1989), Greiner (1972), and Tyebjee et al. (1983).

2. The technical process

The technical process is the method the work group uses to produce its products and/or services. It includes

- The specific requirements for each product or service
- The work flow — the steps a work group takes to produce its products and/or services
- The information flow — the pipeline of information that the group uses to anticipate needs, evaluate operations, and troubleshoot

A work group determines the specific requirements of the technical process by finding out what part of the overall market demand its products and/or services are expected to meet. In addition, the group finds out what role its products and services are expected to play in the organization's overall competitive strategy. The group also examines customer profiles and feedback to anticipate needs and identify expectations.

A work group develops the work flow of the technical process according to customer demands. When customers expect quality, adaptability, customer service, and/or rapid response time, the work flow must be streamlined, unfragmented, and adaptable. To create this kind of work flow, the group must first map out the most direct path from the customer's need to a need-satisfying product or service. Then they must streamline, simplify, and error-proof this path. This typically involves eliminating gaps, stalls, redundancies, and any other non–value adding steps from the current work process. It also involves building in ways for employees to detect and correct common problems at their source.

A work group develops an effective path for information flow by examining how the entire process works. A streamlined process typically relies on employees to do their own planning, checking, and troubleshooting. This requires a well-targeted information pipeline that gives them the information they need to plan, adapt, and troubleshoot on the spot. To create this pipeline, the group must first identify the information that's needed at each planning and decision-making point. Then they must identify the most appropriate channel to move the information where it's needed, when it's needed. This typically involves finding and fixing problems with the existing information flow. It also typically involves opening direct information channels between employees and their internal or external customers.

3. The human structure and support systems

The human structure and support systems determine the way people are organized, controlled, and rewarded. They consist of an organization's

- Structures, lines of authority, and coordination mechanisms: These determine how people are organized, directed, and coordinated.
- Job design: This determines how work gets distributed into individual jobs.
- Human resource systems: These determine how people are selected, trained, evaluated, compensated, rewarded, and disciplined.
- Values and norms: These determine what gets rewarded (both formally and informally) and reflect what people believe is important.

Structures. To support a streamlined, unfragmented process, a work group must include employees from each specialty that contributes to its process. To get the right people on its team, a work group must compare its current makeup to the list of contributors to its process. It must find ways to include those contributors who aren't currently on the team.

Lines of authority and coordination mechanisms. To create a streamlined process, a work group minimizes or eliminates rework. To do this, employees must have the authority to check and troubleshoot their own work. Those who are nearest to the line of action must be able to respond. They must also be able to coordinate their interfaces with other groups. To create this kind of authority structure, employees must first compare the tasks they're responsible for to the issues they have the authority to act on. They must then work with their managers to align their responsibilities with their authority. To find effective mechanisms to coordinate their interfaces, they must first determine how complex and unpredictable those interfaces tend to be. When the interface is simple and predictable, they can coordinate it through mechanisms like standard operating procedures and contacts between interfacing managers. When the interface is complex or unpredictable, they need to coordinate it through direct contact between doers or by redrawing boundaries between work groups (this could include overlapping groups, as in matrix organizations). (Based on Galbraith's [1977] coordination decision criteria.)

Job design. To support flexible processes in which employees take responsibility for planning, checking, and troubleshooting their own work, jobs typically need to be more comprehensive. They need to integrate thinking with doing, and support with production. They also need to provide ownership and challenge. To create these kinds of jobs, the work group typically assesses its current jobs and enriches them so that each job provides

- Variety, by using a broader range of skills
- Identity, by creating a whole product or service or at least a meaningful part
- Significance, by creating something that makes a difference to others
- Autonomy, by providing individual discretion and responsibility
- Intrinsic feedback, so that employees can tell from the work itself how well they're doing

(Based on Hackman and Oldham's [1980] principles of motivating work.)

Human resource systems. To support more comprehensive jobs, employees and managers need new skills. To create the necessary support systems for these enlarged jobs, work groups need to first identify the skill requirements for each job. Employees typically need technical, managerial, administrative, and interpersonal skills. Managers typically need coaching, strategic, and resource-brokering skills. After a work group identifies needed skills it will work with human resources specialists to create selection, training, feedback, and reward systems to build and maintain these skills.

Values and norms. To develop a fast, flat, flexible group, members must value ownership, initiative, growth, adaptability, and teamwork. Not only must the group's leader model and reinforce these values, the feedback and reward system must reinforce them as well. This means the work group must identify critical practices that demonstrate these values and find ways to measure and reward them.

Summary of Key Points

- Organizations face demands for more specialized products and services of better quality, supported by better customer service, in less time, all with fewer resources.

- Past approaches to improving organizational performance have fragmented work and have addressed only slices of whole systems.

- These approaches have resulted in diseconomies of scale, alienation from work, and sagging productivity.

- Dissatisfaction with human outcomes typically precedes inadequate business performance.

- Training practitioners often mistakenly try to fix bad systems by improving the performance of contributors. This doesn't work.

- Human performance technologists align and fix whole systems.

- A whole system consists of

    — The environment and the demands and goals it triggers

    — The technical process—how things get done

    — The human structure and support systems—how people are organized, how work gets distributed, and what gets rewarded

- The purpose of the kind of design this book presents is to create a streamlined, self-regulating system that meets or exceeds environmental demands as it builds employee ownership and initiative.

- A well-designed work process is streamlined and unfragmented. It is supported by an information flow that provides doers with an accurate picture of customer needs and process performance.

- A well-designed work group includes players with the depth and variety of skills necessary to create a whole product or service. The group's authority structure gives employees the autonomy and self-control to respond to needs and problems nearest to the line of action.

- A well-designed job is organized around a whole product or service. It unites thinking with doing, and support with core production. It provides the jobholder direct contact with the customer.

- The result of all this design is: better coordination and information flow; reduced costs and cycle times; more innovation and greater flexibility; and more value added through people.

- Design an organic, involvement-building system whenever: an organization's environment is changing; its strategy requires growth, innovation, or improved quality or service; and its workers must make midprocess adjustments.

For More Information

Resources on business growth cycles and corresponding environmental challenges

Adizes, I. *Corporate Lifecycles*. Englewood Cliffs, N.J.: Prentice Hall, 1988.

Brandt, S. *Entrepreneuring: Ten Commandments for Building a Growth Company*. New York: New American Library, 1982.

Churchill, N. and Lewis, V. "The Five Stages of Small Business Growth," *Harvard Business Review,* May–June, 1983.

Davidow, W. and Uttal, B. *Total Customer Service: The Ultimate Weapon*. New York: Harper Perennial, 1989.

Greiner, L. E. "Evolution and Revolution as Organizations Grow." *Harvard Business Review,* July–August 1972, 41.

Miller, L. *Barbarians to Bureaucrats: Corporate Life Cycle Strategies*. New York: Fawcett Columbine, 1989.

Tyebjee, T., Bruno, A., and McIntyre, S. "Growing Ventures Can Anticipate Marketing Stages." *Harvard Business Review,* January–February, 1983.

Woodward, H. and Buchholz, S. *Aftershock: Helping People Through Corporate Change*. New York: Wiley, 1987.

Resources on the fragmentation of work and job redesign

Cunningham, B. and Eberle, T. "A Guide to Job Enrichment and Redesign." *Personnel,* February, 1990.

Hackman, J. R. and Oldham, G. R. *Work Redesign*. Reading, Mass.: Addison-Wesley, 1980.

Hammer, M. and Champy, J. *Reengineering the Corporation*. New York: Harper Business, 1993.

Lawler, E. E. *The Ultimate Advantage*. San Francisco: Jossey-Bass, 1992.

Rummler, G. A. and Brache, A. P. *Improving Performance: How to Manage the White Space on the Organization Chart*. San Francisco: Jossey-Bass, 1990.

Terkel, S. *Working*. New York: Avon Books, 1974.

Tomasko, R. *Rethinking the Corporation*. New York: AMACOM, 1993.

Resources on organizational design

Galbraith, J. R. *Organization Design*. Reading, Mass.: Addison-Wesley, 1977.

Hanna, D. P. *Designing Organizations for High Performance*. Reading, Mass.: Addison-Wesley, 1988.

Hammer, M. and Champy, J. *Reengineering the Corporation*. New York: Harper Business, 1993.

Lawler, E. E. *The Ultimate Advantage*. San Francisco: Jossey-Bass, 1992.

Lytle, W. O. *Socio-Technical Systems Analysis and Design Guide for Linear Work*. Plainfield, N.J.: Block Petrella Weisbord, 1991.

Lytle, W. O. *Socio-Technical Systems Analysis and Design Guide for Non-Linear Work*. Plainfield, N.J.: Block Petrella Weisbord, 1991.

Meyers, C. *Improving Whole Systems: A Guidebook*. Plainfield, N.J.: Block Petrella Weisbord, 1992.

Miller, L. M. *Design for Total Quality: A Workbook for Socio-Technical Design*. Atlanta: Miller Consulting Group, 1991.

Mintzberg, H. *Structure in Fives: Designing Effective Organizations*. Englewood Cliffs, N.J.: Prentice Hall, 1993.

Mohrman, S. A. and Cummings, T. G. *Self-Designing Organizations*. Reading, Mass.: Addison-Wesley, 1989.

Morgan, G. *Images of Organization*. Newbury Park, Calif.: Sage, 1986.

Morgan, G. *Imaginization*. Newbury Park, Calif.: Sage, 1993.

Nadler, D., Gerstein, M., Shaw, R., et al. *Organizational Architecture: Designs Changing Organizations*. San Francisco: Jossey-Bass, 1992.

Nadler, D. and Tushman, M. *Strategic Organizational Design: Concepts, Tools, & Processes*. New York: HarperCollins, 1988.

Pasmore, W. *Designing Effective Organizations: The Sociotechnical Systems Perspective*. New York: Wiley, 1988.

Rummler, G. A. and Brache, A. P. *Improving Performance*. San Francisco: Jossey-Bass, 1990.

Tomasko, R. *Rethinking the Corporation*. New York: AMACOM, 1993.

Resources on process design and management

Chang, R. Y. "Continuous Process Improvement." *Info-Line,* October 1992.

Davenport, T. *Process Innovation.* Boston: Harvard Business School Press, 1993.

Goal/QPC. *The Memory Jogger: A Pocket Guide of Tools for Continuous Improvement.* Methuen, Mass.: Goal/QPC, 1988.

Hammer, M. "Reengineering Work: Don't Automate, Obliterate." *Harvard Business Review,* July–August, 1990.

Hammer, M. and Champy, J. *Reengineering the Corporation.* New York: Harper Business, 1993.

Harbour, J. L. "Improving Work Processes." *Performance and Instruction,* February 1993.

Harrington, H. J. *Business Process Improvement.* New York: McGraw-Hill, 1991.

Lynch, R. and Cross, K. *Measure Up! Yardsticks for Continuous Improvement.* Cambridge, Mass.: Blackwell Business, 1991.

Miller, L. M. *Design for Total Quality: A Workbook for Socio-Technical Design.* Atlanta: Miller Consulting Group, 1991.

Miller, L. M. and Howard, J. *Managing Quality Through Teams.* Atlanta: Miller Consulting Group, 1991.

Pasmore, W. *Designing Effective Organizations: The Sociotechnical Systems Perspective.* New York: Wiley, 1988.

Robson, G. *Continuous Process Improvement: Simplifying Work Flow Systems.* New York: Free Press, 1991.

Rummler, G. A. and Brache, A. P. *Improving Performance.* San Francisco: Jossey-Bass, 1990.

Rummler, G. A. and Brache, A. P. "Managing the White Space." *Training,* January 1991.

Resource on performance technology overall

Stolovich, K. *Handbook of Human Performance Technology.* San Francisco: Jossey-Bass, 1992

TECHNIQUES FOR DESIGNING WORK GROUPS AND JOBS

Overview

Purpose of this section

Section One defined systems and their components, described problems of misaligned systems, and listed benefits and principles of design. This section explains how to apply the principles from Section One to the design of a single work group's processes, composition, and individual jobs. The procedures in this section provide the tools to

1. *initiate and scope* the design project

2. *analyze* the current system (i.e., work group)

3. *design* a new and better system

4. *implement* the new system

In case-study fashion, examples are used throughout Section Two to show how the procedures are used and what the possible results might look like.

The heart of this book mimics the heart of any design effort. Therefore, greater coverage is given to analysis and design than to initiation, scoping, and implementation. Yet, those activities are important enough to warrant their own chapters and procedures.

How to use this section

Initiation and scoping. Chapter 2 describes procedures to allow you to help a manager and work group decide if they should even begin a design project. If it's decided that design is the appropriate intervention, the chapter provides guidance in how to establish a design project's purpose and scope. Here is where you define desired outcomes and make a preliminary assessment of the current system before scoping the overall design project.

Analysis. Chapters 3, 4, and 5 will help you uncover the current system's strengths and weaknesses. These chapters—Defining the Purpose and Scope of the Redesign Effort; Environmental Analysis: Identifying Critical Goals, Demands, and Constraints; and Technical Process Analysis: Understanding How the Group Creates Its Products and Services—present the order in which you will analyze the current system. This sequence of analysis allows the data to build on itself as you proceed. The procedures allow you to find out what is and is not working in the current system. By analyzing the existing system you

- Establish a baseline from which to measure future progress
- Preserve what's working in the existing system
- Change only what needs changing
- Prepare stakeholders to let go of the past and take ownership of the design process

Design. Relying on the results from the analysis phase, you follow the procedures in Chapters 6 through 8 to guide the work group in designing an improved and fully functioning system. These chapters mirror those from the analysis phase. This will allow the design to impact the significant problems you uncover while analyzing the system. Here you create whole systems whose parts *together* produce a result that's greater than the sum of what each part could contribute on its own. A well-designed system can result in

- Better anticipation and responsiveness to customer needs
- Better adaptation to environmental changes
- Higher-quality products and services
- Reduced costs and cycle times
- Better coordination and information flow
- More flexibility and innovation
- Better esprit de corps

Implementation. Chapter 9 allows you and the work group to plan how to set the design in motion. Once it's planned, you're guided in the steps of implementation, when you operationalize the design.

Analysis and Design: The Heart of Work-Group and Job Design

The importance of analysis and design cannot be overstated. The success of the effort will depend on these two activities. A closer examination of how these phases of work-group and job design occur will make this clear.

Analysis

Analysis involves examining the same three kinds of factors that you examine in a preliminary assessment. However, this analysis will be more comprehensive and systematic than the preliminary analysis. Specifically, you will examine

1. **The environment** and the demands and goals that it triggers. This includes

   - Groups and forces that are outside of the immediate work group, but influence it (such as external or internal customers and suppliers)

   - Business strategies, goals, and objectives

2. **The technical process**. This includes

   - Work flow

   - Information flow

   - Product or service requirements and deficiencies

3. **The human structure and support systems**. This includes

   - Structure, lines of authority, and coordination mechanisms: how people are organized, directed, and coordinated

   - Job design: how work gets distributed into individual jobs

   - Human resource systems: how people are selected, trained, evaluated, compensated, rewarded, and disciplined

   - Values and norms: what gets rewarded (both formally and informally), as well as what people believe is important

Analysis at this level will include process mapping and error tracking, in addition to the kinds of opinion data included in the preliminary analysis. If that sounds time-consuming, it can be! That's why it's important to narrow the design project's scope to the "critical few" processes that make the most difference in accomplishing the desired outcomes. (If you skip project scoping, you could be in for analysis paralysis!)

How do you get involved?

There are three types of circumstances under which you should perform an analysis:

1. After the work group manager and members have reached agreement about the design project's purpose and scope

2. Periodically after you have implemented a design, to see how well it is accomplishing what you planned

3. Whenever the environment, technology, work structure, or labor pool changes significantly

What's required to analyze the existing work system?

To analyze the existing work system, the work group must

- Identify customers, suppliers, and other outside influences

- Estimate their needs and impact on the future

- Track the steps and path that the work group takes to create its products and services

- Break the organization down into work groups and their tasks into jobs.

- Evaluate the authority structure and support systems to ensure they reinforce doers in taking action

How is the analysis phase organized?

To perform these activities:	Read this chapter:
• Define desired outcomes • Make a preliminary assessment • Draft the purpose and scope of the design project	Chapter 2 — Defining the Purpose and Scope of the Redesign Effort
• Finalize the purpose and scope of the design project • Identify outside influences on the work group • Estimate customer requirements • Determine levels of customer satisfaction • Set goals and objectives for future work processes	Chapter 3 — Environmental Analysis: Identifying Critical Goals, Demands, and Constraints
• Track the path that the work group takes to create its products and services	Chapter 4 — Technical Process Analysis: Understanding How the Group Creates Its Products and Services
• Examine the organization of people and jobs • Evaluate the authority structure and support systems	Chapter 5 — Human Systems Analysis: Understanding How People and Jobs Are Organized and Supported

Design

Getting a better system usually requires the work group to design a new system and *not* simply patch up their old one. As the old saying goes, "If you do what you've always done, you'll get what you've always gotten." The more paths the work group considers to meet customer needs, the more robust the ultimate design can become. To ignite the spark of creativity and generate a variety of solutions, you need to break out of the "logic boxes" that constrain the way things have always been done. The more you break free of existing assumptions, the greater the likelihood that you can greatly improve existing performance.

The greatest risk of design is the failure to generate options that are different enough from the current system that they justify the effort involved to change. This "small change" risk is especially high at this point in the design process, because team members have become accustomed to the convergent, analytic thinking they've been using to describe the current system. Design, on the other hand, involves divergent, creative thinking, to imagine a new system. In the design chapters you will see how to serve as a catalyst to the design process. You'll see how to guide the work group in designing

1. Goals that meet the demands of their environment

2. A technical process that's fast, focused, and unfragmented

3. Human structures and systems that reinforce initiative and teamwork and build competence and flexibility

How do you get involved?

There are three types of circumstances under which the work group may begin designing a new system:

1. Once the work group has performed all of the procedures in the analysis phase.

2. After the group has identified problems with a newly designed system. (In this case, redesign only those elements that aren't working.)

3. When reengineering has occurred within the work group's division (or other superordinate level). Reengineering often makes the existing system obsolete, so it's usually more efficient to design a new system than to modify the existing one.

What's required to design a work system?

To design a work system you

1. Set goals to meet your environmental demands

2. Design a technical process to meet your goals

3. Design human structures and systems that reinforce your goals and fit with your environment, technical process, and work force.

How is the design phase organized?

To perform these activities:	Read this chapter:
• Set goals for the design • Determine the scope of the design	Chapter 6 — Goal Design: Matching Work Group Goals to Environmental Demands
• Challenge assumptions and generate alternatives to the current process • Design a new work flow • Set specifications and measures for products and services • Develop an improved information flow	Chapter 7 — Technical Process Design: Building Speed, Focus, and Integration into the Flow of Work
• Identify the effect change will have on structure, authority, and coordination • Design new structure and authority and coordination mechanisms • Select appropriate job-design options • Draft selection criteria, feedback, assessment, and reward systems • Design selection practices and training systems • Finalize human structures and systems design specifications	Chapter 8 — Human Systems Design: Building Initiative and Teamwork into Jobs
• Draft action plans • Finalize action plans • Implement and consolidate action plans	Chapter 9 — Implementation: Managing the Transition from Plans to Reality

CHAPTER 2

Defining the Purpose and Scope of the Redesign Effort

To initiate and scope a design project, you must help a manager and a work group define what they hope to produce and estimate what's getting in the way of producing it. If they decide that process-related problems are getting in the way, help them set the purpose and scope of the design project. If they determine the process is *not* the problem, you can recommend another intervention, like training.

If you're asked to provide training for problems that seem intrinsic to the way the work is done, you're probably facing process-related problems. These problems tend to occur across the work group, affecting good and bad performers alike. Their symptoms include

- Slow cycle times

- Poor product or service quality

- Poor responsiveness or insufficient capacity to act

- Conflict across performers

- Apparent incompetence across appropriately qualified and rewarded performers

When problems seem to be process-related or when reorganization, reengineering, or design has been completed at a higher level, it's appropriate to assess the work's design.

Purpose of this chapter

This chapter explains how to help a manager and work group decide whether to begin a design project. It also explains how to establish a design project's purpose and scope. Initiation and scoping provide a first-cut analysis of the current system. Even at this preliminary stage, analysis involves looking at three factors:

1. **The environment** and the demands and goals that it triggers

2. **The technical process** — how things get done

3. **The human structure and support systems** — how people are organized, how work gets distributed, and what gets rewarded

How is this chapter organized?

To perform these activities:	Follow this procedure:
• Describe an ideal future work process • Identify desired business results • Determine desired quality of work life • Reconcile conflicts between desired quality of work life and desired business results	Procedure 2.1 — Define Desired Outcomes
• Compare actual product and service results to planned results • Estimate customer requirements • Estimate supplier requirements • Estimate current quality of work life • Identify gaps between current and estimated requirements and outcomes	Procedure 2.2 — Make a Preliminary Assessment
• Identify the most important shortfalls in the system • Set objectives for what should be produced as a result of the processes • Describe the tasks and roles involved in the design process • Identify resources and constraints that could impact the design process • Draft purpose and scope	Procedure 2.3 — Draft the Purpose and Scope of the Design Project

To perform these activities:	Follow this procedure:
• Review 　—Critical process problems. 　—Objectives for business results 　—Work processes selected for design 　—Resources and constraints 　—Identify ways to overcome obstacles and constraints to design 　—Reach consensus on processes to change • Identify ways to overcome obstacles and constraints to design • Reach consensus on process to change	Procedure 2.4 — Finalize the Purpose and Scope of the Design Project

As you saw above, the first procedure has the work group define its desired outcomes. Then the group makes a preliminary assessment of its current process. It's important to note the reason for this: If you begin a design project with a focus on problems, you limit the parameters around which the design will be based. In other words, you end up looking only at the deficiencies and problems in the process. But if you start with a focus on outcomes, you're free of any such parameters. You are free to consider all the possibilities, all the what-ifs, in deciding what a new process will look like. In addition, when you start by visioning, you allow the group to start out with positive, proactive thinking. In contrast, when you start by defining problems, you can start the group out with negative, defensive thinking.

Meetings

A predesign conference and three sets of meetings are required to design the human structures and support systems. The table below explains their sequence and purposes.

Meet with:	In this sequence:	To focus on:
The work group's manager	First (the predesign conference)	Preparing the manager to discuss structures and distribution of authority with his or her group
Expanded group	Second	Structure, authority, and coordination mechanisms
Expanded group	Third	Job design
Expanded group	Fourth	Setting design specifications

Results

Once the procedures in this chapter are complete, you will have achieved the following outcomes:

- A clear picture of what's desired
- A management decision on whether design is necessary and whether the work group's current system can produce the desired outcomes
- A management decision on whether the system needs fine-tuning or an overhaul
- A clear and compelling vision that will inspire hope and generate collective support for change
- Participant commitment to the design process
- Definition of the design project's purpose and scope
- A preliminary project timeline

For More Information

Beckhard, R. and Harris, R. T. *Organizational Transitions: Managing Complex Change*. Reading, Mass.: Addison-Wesley, 1987. Chapter 4, "The Change Process: Why Change?" describes how to define the importance and urgency of forces driving the change (pp. 29–44). Chapter 5, "Defining the Future State," describes how to identify the vision, or ultimate goal, of change as well as midpoint goals (pp. 45–56).

Block, P. *Flawless Consulting*. Austin, Texas: Learning Concepts, 1981. Chapters 4, "Contracting Overview"; 5, "The Contracting Meeting"; and 6, "The Agonies of Contracting," describe the contracting process (pp. 41–103).

Hanna, D. P. *Designing Organizations for High Performance*. Reading, Mass.: Addison-Wesley, 1988. Pages 49–51 describe the assessment process.

Lytle, W. O. *Starting an Organization Design Effort*. Plainfield, N.J.: Block Petrella Weisbord, 1993. Chapter 1, "Need: Determining Why Change Is Necessary," describes how to determine need (pp. 1–12). Chapter 2, "Vision: Deciding What the Organization Needs to Be," describes how to establish a vision (pp. 21–26). Chapter 5, "The Charter: Developing a Project Statement," describes how to establish the design project's purpose (pp. 77–104).

Miller, L. M. *Design for Total Quality*. Atlanta: Miller Consulting Group, 1991. Chapter 4, "Writing the Charter," describes how to write a purpose statement (pp. 87–102).

Miller, L. M. and Howard, J. *Managing Quality Through Teams*. Atlanta: Miller Consulting Group, 19xx. Chapter 2, "Customer Focus," describes how to determine customer requirements (pp. 31–42).

Mohrman, S. A. and Cummings, T. G. *Self-Designing Organizations*. Reading, Mass.: Addison-Wesley, 1989. Chapter 5, "Valuing," describes how to establish vision and values (pp. 59–66).

| Procedure 2.1 | ## Define Desired Outcomes |

Purpose of this procedure

As Bob Mager (1984) has warned, "If you're not sure where you're going, you're liable to end up someplace else." This is as true for process and work design as it is for instructional design. To define desired outcomes, help the manager and work group to envision what they want for the future. Include both business results and desired quality of work life. Business results address customer expectations (such as product or service quantity, quality, and timeliness). Desired quality of work life addresses employee needs (such as their need for information, feedback, and stimulating work).

When to use this procedure

Clients may ask you to develop training to address problems that typically occur at predictable "problem spots" in the product or service cycle, regardless of the skills or experience of the performer. These conditions often indicate process-related problems. Symptoms include

- Work flows that don't flow. Work that gets bogged down or disappears into bureaucratic "black holes."

- Work that "slips between the cracks" when it passes to other work groups.

- Decisions based on factors that have little to do with customer satisfaction (such as the way things have always been done).

- Fragmented products or services (when the work group's work flow produces only a fragment of the product or service, such as tightened screws or marked-up documents).

- Responsibility without corresponding authority (such as when work group members must adjust to changes in inputs but aren't allowed to change standard operating procedures).

- Ongoing, unresolved conflict. (Problems that, at first glance, appear to be personality clashes are often, upon closer examination, due to inadequate structures and systems.)

When a client asks for advice or training to fix problems that seem process-related, it's a good idea to involve the manager and work group in defining what results they'd like to see. Your role is to facilitate creative, freewheeling meetings that stimulate contributors to imagine themselves and their work process at its best.

Before you start

1. Have the work group's manager list the parameters that will determine or constrain desired outcomes, such as

   - The internal or external customer groups the work group must serve
   - Customer requirements for the products or services the group produces
   - Business strategies and objectives the group must support
   - Nonnegotiable resource limitations

2. Prepare for a brainstorming meeting. Create an activity that gets the group to visualize what success will look like five years into the future. (Two good books on brainstorming activities are *Idea Power* by Arthur B. Van Gundy [New York: AMACOM, 1992], and *Thinkertoys* by Michael Michalko [Berkeley, Calif.: Ten Speed Press, 1991]. Another classic is *The Winning Trainer* by Julius E. Eitington [Houston: Gulf, 1989].)

3. Schedule a meeting and inform participants the purpose is to imagine what's possible in their work process, without limiting themselves to what currently exists.

What to do

Steps	Specifics
1. Make sure the group understands all work-related parameters and limits.	Ask the manager to present all the parameters he or she listed before the meeting. Facilitate questions or concerns.
2. Generate initial descriptions of an ideal future work process.	Have participants imagine they are successful in accomplishing everything they hope to accomplish and in supporting the organization's business strategy. Ask them to describe what they're producing and what the work process will look, sound, and feel like.

3. Determine the business results the group hopes to accomplish over the next year or two.	Ask these questions:
	
	• What customer groups do you want to serve?
	
	• What products and/or services do you want to provide for each customer group?
	
	• What customer requirements do you anticipate?
	
	• What competitive advantage (or unique selling position) do you want your products and services to have compared to your competitors'?
	
	• What performance indicators are most critical to meeting requirements and maintaining a competitive advantage? Consider
	
	   —Quality
	   —Quantity
	   —Timeliness (cycle time)
	   —Consistency
	   —Productivity
	   —Flexibility
	   —Customer satisfaction

Steps	Specifics
4. Determine the quality of work life that will best support the desired business results over the next one to two years.	Ask these questions: • How quickly and often must you change your work routines to respond to your customers? • How complex is your work and the technology you use to do it? • How interdependent are the parts that you each contribute to your collective products or services? • How much growth do you look for in your job? How long can you do an average job within this work group without becoming bored?
5. Reconcile any conflicts between the quality of work life that the group desires and the group's desired business results.	In cases with conflicting outcomes, ask the group to agree on which conflicting outcomes must be resolved to support the group's desired business results.
6. Compare the desired business results and the desired quality of work life with the parameters that the manager compiled before the meeting.	List any conflicts. Negotiate changes to parameters or outcomes as necessary to reconcile conflicts.
7. Document all findings.	

Exhibit 2.1 describes the procedure's steps and the type of documentation that might result from each one.

Exhibit 2.1 Defining Desired Outcomes

Steps	Information to Gather	Documentation
2	Process results	Generic list of hoped-for results
3	Business results	
3.1	Customer groups to be serviced	Specific group names, demographic information
3.2	Product or services to be provided by group	Specific goals. Each group must be included or dropped from list in 3.1
3.3	Customer requirements	Special requirements that make the group unique
3.4	Competitive advantage(s)	A list
3.5	Performance indicators	A list. May include quality, quantity, timeliness, consistency, or other attributes that would provide a competitive edge
4	Internal quality of work-life conditions	
4.1	Adaptability	Identification of anticipated need to adjust production speed or nature of deliverables.
4.2	Complexity	List of equipment, software, and process steps (with branches)
4.3	Interdependencies	List of who must rely on whom and in what way(s).
4.4	Growth needs	
5	Reconciliation of what the group wants and what seems to be required	List of incompatibilities
6	Comparison of results of this process with what was expected before these results were generated	List of conflicts and requirements for resolving them

Make a Preliminary Assessment

Purpose of this procedure

Designing work processes, groups, and jobs takes time, money, and the involvement of the entire work team as well as its suppliers and customers. To decide whether to make an in-depth analysis, the team and its manager need to make an initial estimate of how well the current design is working. If there's little dissatisfaction and the existing design looks adequate to meet anticipated requirements, there's no need to go forward. If there's significant dissatisfaction and/or the existing design looks inadequate to meet anticipated requirements, then it's worth it to make a more in-depth analysis. By involving suppliers and customers in making this assessment, you prompt them to voice their dissatisfaction as well, and you build momentum among work group members for change.

Your assessment should provide the work team's manager with the information he or she needs to decide whether to make the more thorough analysis that the design process requires. If this preliminary analysis reveals many shortfalls, advise the manager that it's often more efficient and productive to design a whole new work process than it is to patch up each of the individual problems with the current system.

When to use this procedure

After the team has identified the outcomes they'd like to see, it's time to help them compare those outcomes to the ones they're currently achieving. In addition, whenever design, reengineering, or restructuring occurs within the work group's division, it's appropriate to do a preliminary assessment of the work group.

Before you start

1. Compile this documentation

   • Procedure 2.1 data

   • Existing plans, records, and reports about the work group's products and services

2. Determine

   • What products and/or services the group offers

   • Who its customers are, what they need and expect, and how satisfied they currently are

   • What goals or objectives currently exist for these products and services

   • How important they are to the organization's overall business strategy

3. Gather only as much information as you need to make an educated guess about the current design's adequacy. This should *not* involve detailed observation, formal sampling, or surveying.

4. Schedule interviews to ask the work group's manager, experienced work group members, and a few representative customers and suppliers to assess the current system. Emphasize that the purpose of this information gathering is to get a rough idea of whether the way they're doing things now will get them where they want to go, and that consequently the interviews will focus on what's happening, *not* on who's to blame. NOTE: If time is short, you may substitute a focus group of experienced work group members instead of interviewing each individual member.

5. Develop a timetable to complete this procedure.

What to do

Steps	Specifics
1. Compare actual results to planned results.	Ask the work group manager and experienced members this question: • Are the products or services reaching the goals or objectives that were set for them?
2. Estimate current and anticipated customer requirements.	Ask the work group manager and customers these questions: • What does the internal or external customer require from the product or service? • Given current trends, what will they expect in the future?
3. Compare current products and services to customer requirements.	Ask the manager, customers, and work group members these questions: • Do the current products and services satisfy your current requirements? Will they satisfy your future requirements? • If not, what product/service specifications need to change?
4. List current and anticipated supplier requirements (what the work group requires from their internal or external suppliers).	Ask the work group manager and experienced members these questions: • What input specifications do you set for your suppliers? • What input specifications will you set in the future?

(continued on next page)

Steps	Specifics
5. Compare your suppliers' current inputs to your current and future specifications.	Ask the work group manager and experienced members these questions: • Does your supplier consistently meet your current specifications? • Will the supplier be able to consistently meet your anticipated specifications in the future? • If not, what input specifications need to change?
6. Estimate current and anticipated supplier capabilities and needs.	Ask suppliers and the work group manager these questions: • Are supplies consistently provided on time and to specification? • Are the supply chain requirements fair? • If not, what needs to be changed?
7. Estimate current and anticipated quality of work life (such as safety, retention, work satisfaction, professional growth, and employee involvement and initiative).	Ask experienced work group members these questions: • How involved are employees in making decisions about their products or services? • How much initiative do they take in preventing, spotting, and resolving problems? • How well do their jobs support professional growth, satisfaction, and retention? • Given trends in your environment and labor pool, how satisfactory will the quality of work life in your group be in the future?

Steps	Specifics
8. Compare current quality of work life to desired quality of work life (identified in the previous procedure, "Define Desired Outcomes").	Ask the work group's manager and experienced team members these questions: • What changes in quality of work life are needed to adjust to anticipated changes in customer expectations, work tasks, and the labor force? • How do these changes compare with the current situation?
9. List any gaps — areas in which current performance will *not* support anticipated requirements or desired quality of work life.	Ask work group manager and members this question: • In what areas do current results fall short of desired results?
10. Determine other process-related problems or performance issues respondents are aware of.	Ask the work group manager and members this question: • Have other problems occurred in your day-to-day work that, in retrospect, appear to be connected to the issues that you've identified here?

Exhibit 2.2 identifies the primary and secondary sources of information for this procedure.

Exhibit 2.2 Preliminary Assessment Matrix

Activity	Manager	Work Group	Suppliers	Customers
Compare actual results to planned results.	Primary source	Secondary source		
Estimate customer requirements.	Secondary source			Primary source
Compare current products or services to customer requirements.	Secondary source	Secondary source		Primary source
Identify requirements for suppliers.	Secondary source	Primary source		
Judge quality of supplier inputs.		Primary source	Secondary source	
Specify current conditions and quality of work life.	Secondary source	Primary source		
List anticipated conditions and quality of work life.	Secondary source	Primary source		
Determine gaps between current and anticipated quality of work life.	Secondary source	Primary source		
List other process-related problems or anticipated problems.	Primary source	Primary source	Secondary source	Secondary source

| Procedure 2.3 | **Draft the Purpose and Scope of the Design Project** |

Purpose of this procedure

During the preliminary assessment the work group will probably have uncovered lots of ways the current system fails to reach its desired outcomes. Now you must get the work group's manager to prioritize these problems and identify the work processes they affect. Since you rarely have time to redesign all the work processes the work group uses, it's important to find the "critical few" that matter the most to meeting customers' needs. After the manager has identified the processes of most concern, you can help him or her determine project goals, resources, and constraints.

When to use this procedure

Use this procedure once a work group's manager has decided to proceed with a design project. But make sure that you're clear on the outcomes the manager and team expect from the project. Never embark on designing a work system without first reaching agreement on expectations. In addition, as you proceed with the design process, whenever things change significantly enough to invalidate the existing agreement, you should renegotiate and revise the project's purpose and scope.

Terms you may not know

The difference between work process and group process:

Work process How the work group produces its products or services. A sequence of steps and/or decisions that results in a product or service.

Group process How the work group establishes and maintains interpersonal relationships. The interpersonal methods group members use to communicate with each other.

Before you start

1. Review your notes about desired versus actual outcomes. List the most important ways in which the current system fails to produce the work group's desired outcomes.

2. Ask the work group's manager to set aside time for two half-day meetings and a single two-hour meeting. In the two half-day meetings you will work one-on-one with the manager to determine the project's purpose and scope. In the two-hour meeting, the manager and work group members will review the project's purpose and scope and suggest any adjustments they believe are necessary.

3. Have the manager bring to the first meeting:

   • Goals and expectations he or she has of the design process

   • Criteria that will indicate when goals have been accomplished

   • A list of available project resources and constraints

   • A calendar of events that could impact the design process

4. Scan this book to identify the design tasks that the design process will involve. (For a list of design factors, see the introduction to Section Two of this book.) Establish your own estimates of how long it will take to do these tasks in your organization. Typically this kind of process can take from six to eighteen months or more, depending on the size of the work group, the seriousness of the problems, and the comprehensiveness of the design project.

5. Develop a timetable to schedule and complete these meetings.

What to do

In the two half-day meetings with the work group's manager:

1. Share your list of the most important ways that the current system fails to produce desired outcomes.

   Ask if he or she sees these as the most important shortfalls.

   Revise the list as he or she suggests.

2. Ask the manager to identify the work processes in which each of these problems occurs.

3. Identify high-impact, significant processes.

   Ask the manager to select process(es) that:

   - Are *least* effective and efficient at producing desired outcomes.

   - Have the greatest impact on external customer satisfaction.

   - Provide the best balance of potential payoff and success. The more you change the way things are done in the current system, the *higher* the potential payoff, but the *lower* the probability of success.

4. Help the manager set objectives for what these processes should produce in order to reach desired business results.

5. Ask the manager to identify the quality of work life that is most critical to meeting the objectives in the previous step.

   Help the manager set objectives for quality of work life.

(continued on next page)

6. Describe for the manager the tasks and roles that the design process typically involves.	For a list of design tasks, see the introduction to Section Two of this book.
7. Ask the manager to identify resources and constraints that could impact the design process.	Identify the time frame within which the manager expects changes to occur. The process will take more time if you have ambitious objectives, serious problems, or a comprehensive project. The manager's time frame can narrow down the work processes that the project addresses.
8. Identify concerns about the objectives, roles, resources, and constraints that have been identified.	Ask the manager how comfortable he or she is with this purpose and scope agreement.
	Jointly agree upon ways to address the concerns.
	Make sure you are comfortable with the manager's level of commitment.
	If it seems that the manager intends to delegate his or her contribution to the design process, call this to his or her attention. Explain that this role *cannot* be delegated.
	If the manager cannot participate, do *not* continue with a design project.

Exhibit 2.3 lists common roles in the design process.

Exhibit 2.3 The Roles in a Design Project

To provide this information, expertise, or authority:	Include this project team member:
Skill in work-system design	Consultant (Typically, *external* consultants who specialize in work design have more experience in the design process than *internal* consultants. If you're relatively inexperienced in work systems design, you may want to work with an external consultant on your first few work design projects.)
Knowledge of the business, politics, and culture of the organization	Sponsor (The work group's manager will typically fill this role.) Internal consultant
Ability to set direction and authorize goals, assignments, and resources	Work group's manager
Knowledge of the information needed to support planning and decision making for the group's work process	Work group's manager
Knowledge of the group's work process	Work team members
Knowledge of customer requirements	Internal or external customer representative
Knowledge of supplier capabilities	Internal or external supplier representative
Knowledge of information systems available to the work group	Information systems representative
Knowledge of the human resource systems that apply to	Internal human resources consultant

| Procedure 2.4 | **Finalize the Purpose and Scope of the Design Project** |

Purpose of this procedure

Reaching agreement on a work design project's scope is very similar to determining the scope of an instructional design project. It is essential to reach agreement on what the work group manager and members expect of the project at its outset. Without this agreement the project is doomed to failure.

Peter Block (1981) calls this the point of maximum leverage for the consultant (pp. 41–103). He says that if you fail to negotiate shared input and control during this stage, you will lose opportunities for impact for the life of the project. Since one of the most important purposes of design is to enable work groups to adapt their processes and systems to changing needs and constraints, it is essential that you establish their ownership at the outset. Only when those who must implement the system have taken an active role in creating it can they provide the support and troubleshooting necessary to overcome the barriers to change that are bound to arise.

In design projects involving large work groups (more than twelve work team members) it's a good idea to spell out your agreements in a design charter. For information on how to construct a design charter see Gelinas and James, *Collaborative Organization Design* (Chap. C-3).

When to use this procedure

Once you have a draft of the project's purpose and scope you are ready to finalize the project plan. To do this you need to help the group negotiate and reach a consensus on the details uncovered in Procedure 2.3. With that done, the group can draft a preliminary project timeline.

Before you start

1. Schedule a meeting and inform participants they will
   - Review and reach a consensus in the project's purpose, scope, and objectives and the roles they will play in the project
   - Consider their manager's resources and constraints in their discussions
   - Create a preliminary project timeline
2. Inform the group that to reach a consensus on an issue, everyone must be able to live with the choice that they're considering. However, a consensus does *not* mean that it must be everyone's first choice. Also let them know that, without a consensus, either the manager's choice will stand or the design project will not go forward. If the project does not go forward, the manager may address problems that the preliminary assessment revealed without necessarily getting the work group's input.

What to do

Steps	Specifics
1. Review and discuss the problems the manager considers most critical.	Ask the work group how they see these problems.
	Revise problem descriptions as needed to reach an agreement between the manager and the work group.
2. Review and discuss the manager's objectives for business results and quality of work life.	Facilitate negotiations between the work group and its manager until they reach consensus on outcomes and objectives.
3. Review and discuss the work processes the manager selected for redesign.	Ask the group whether changing these processes would make enough difference in reaching their desired outcomes to make it worth their time and commitment.
	If not, ask them to identify the processes that *would* justify their efforts.
	Facilitate negotiation between the work group and its manager until they reach a consensus on processes worth changing.
4. Describe the tasks and roles that the design process typically involves.	See Exhibit 2.3.
5. Review and discuss the manager's resources and constraints.	List: • Additional resources and constraints the group is aware of. • Obstacles to fulfilling design project roles.
6. Facilitate problem solving about ways to cope with or overcome obstacles and constraints.	

(continued on next page)

Steps	Specifics
7. Review the manager's calendar of events that could impact the design process.	Facilitate the group in identifying who will contribute to each task. Help the group create a first draft of a project timeline.

Ask members for their commitment to fulfilling their roles. |
| 8. Identify and resolve concerns. | Ask group members how comfortable they are with the agreement.

Jointly agree upon ways to address their concerns.

If it seems that the work team cannot reach an agreement to which they're committed, do *not* continue with a design project. |

Exhibit 2.4 is a gap verification checklist for use in completing this procedure.

Exhibit 2.4   Gap Verification Checklist

Use the date column to record either the date the step was accomplished or (if it's in the future) when you expect it to happen. The comments section is very important in this process. Each full step should be formally documented in some way. Use the comments section to indicate how that documentation was accomplished and how the documents can be retrieved.

Step	Description	Date	Comments
1a	Solicit problem statements from manager.		
1b	Work group — review manager's statements with manager to determine which are most important for him/her.		
2a	Review and discuss (with manager) manager's objectives and aspirations for quality-of-work life.		
2b	Compare manager's priorities with those of the work group.		
2c	Meet with manager to reach consensus in areas where there is disagreement.		
3a	Ask manager to select processes s/he would like to have redesigned.		
3b	Ask work group members if they agree with the manager's assessment. If not, what would they suggest?		
3c	Continue to negotiate in this way until agreement is reached.		
4	Describe the tasks and roles you expect for the design process.		
5a	List resources.		
5b	List constraints.		
6a	Conduct problem solving session(s) as appropriate to develop possible alternatives for action.		
6b	Select (Workgroup as a group) alternative most likely to succeed.		
7a	Review organization, division, and departmental calendars to discover possible time constraints.		
7b	Develop draft of proposed schedule for the project for review by management.		
8	Review all elements so far to ascertain that no problems or concerns remain that may resist resolution.		

CHAPTER 3

Environmental Analysis: Identifying Critical Goals, Demands, and Constraints

To create a better system, a work group must first be clear on what's expected. Expectations can come from internal or external customers, suppliers, regulators, and competitors. These outside influences set the standards the work group must meet or surpass.

Purpose of this chapter

This chapter provides the tools and steps to answer key questions about the environment, demands, and goals:

- Who influences what the work group produces?
- What do they influence, expect, or provide?
- How satisfied are these outside influences with the group's products or services?
- What goals should the work group set in response, both now and for the future?

How is this chapter organized?

To perform these activities:	Follow this procedure:
• Interview/survey customers • Estimate customer requirements • Determine levels of customer satisfaction • Ensure the work group's survey results coincide with the organization's strategic plans	Procedure 3.1 — Determine Customer Requirements and Levels of Satisfaction
• Estimate the impact of outside groups or forces on work group processes • Set goals and objectives for future work processes	Procedure 3.2 — Set Goals and Objectives for Work Processes by Analyzing the Business Environment

Tools to analyze the environment, demands, and goals

The following tools will help the work group gather information about the forces that influence it, those forces' effects or expectations, and the group's resulting goals and objectives.

Structured interview. An interview based on a list of questions. The questions typically ask for opinions about a central issue or concern.

Survey. A list of questions, usually with defined answer categories so you can easily quantify responses. Whenever you believe that interview findings might not be representative of your entire customer population, you may use surveys to find out how representative your interview findings are.

Business environment matrix. A matrix in which you list influential groups or forces, what each one expects, what each one provides, and what goals this suggests, both now and for the future. (See the Business Environment Matrix, Resource A in Section Four.)

NOTE: (If you have no experience in interviewing or survey design, see books such as *Mail and Telephone Surveys: The Total Design Method* by Don Dillman [1978] or *The Competent Manager's Handbook for Measuring Unit Productivity* by Odin Westgaard [1985].)

Results

By analyzing the environment, demands, and goals, the group will reach agreement on

- The demands the group's customers place on it
- The level of satisfaction customers have with the group's products or services
- The group's goals and objectives for the future

Once the group reaches agreement on where it needs to go, it can then examine how it should go about getting there. In the next chapter the group will analyze the technical processes it currently uses to reach its destination.

For More Information

Beckhard, R. and Harris, R. T. *Organizational Transitions: Managing Complex Change* (Reading, Mass.: Addison-Wesley, 1987). Chapter 4, "The Change Process: Why Change?" describes how to define the importance and urgency of forces driving the change (pp. 29–44). Chapter 5, "Defining the Future State," describes how to identify the ultimate goal of change as well as midpoint goals (pp. 45–56). Chapter 6, "Assessing the Present," describes how to define the present state and determine readiness for change (pp. 57–70). Chapter 10, "Commitment Planning and Strategies, Responsibility Charting," describes the responsibility charting process that you will use in this chapter (pp. 104–113).

Dillman, D. *Mail and Telephone Surveys: The Total Design Method* (New York: Wiley, 1978).

Hammer, M. and Champy, J. *Reengineering the Corporation* (New York: Harper Business, 1993). Chapter 3, "Rethinking Business Processes" describes principles of process design (pp. 50–64). Chapter 4, "The New World of Work," describes principles of work design (pp. 65–82).

Hanna, D. P. *Designing Organizations for High Performance* (Reading, Mass.: Addison-Wesley, 1988). Chapter 2, "An Organization Performance Model," and Chapter 3, "The Assessment Process," describe the assessment process (specifically, pp. 45–91).

Kepner, C. H. and Tregoe, B. B. *The New Rational Manager* (Princeton, N.J.: Kepner-Tregoe, 1991). Chapter 2, "Problem Analysis," explains a problem definition process (pp. 32–56).

Lawler, E. E. *The Ultimate Advantage* (San Francisco: Jossey-Bass, 1992). Chapter 2, "Choosing the Right Management Style," explains how to select appropriate design components for the business strategy, environment, work process or technology, and labor force (pp. 25–48).

Lytle, W. O. *Starting an Organization Design Effort* (Plainfield, N. J.: Block Petrella Weisbord, 1993). Chapter 1, "Need: Determining Why Change Is Necessary," describes how to identify need (pp. 1–12).

Lytle, W. O. *Socio-Technical Systems Analysis and Design Guide for Linear Work* (Plainfield, N. J.: Block Petrella Weisbord, 1993). Part 2, "Analysis of the Business Environment," Part 3, "Technical System Analysis" (p. 22), Part 4, "Social System Analysis," and Part 5, "Summary of Analyses," describe, in detail, how to complete this same kind of analysis for an entire business or business division (pp. 5–98).

Mohrman, S. A. and Cummings, T. G. *Self-Designing Organizations* (Reading, Mass.: Addison-Wesley, 1989). Chapter 6, "Diagnosing," describes how to identify gaps between the current and desired situation (pp. 67–84).

Westgaard, O. and Hale, J. *The Competent Manager's Handbook for Measuring Unit Productivity* (Chicago: Hale Associates, 1985) describes components of survey and interview design.

| Procedure 3.1 | **Determine Customer Requirements and Levels of Satisfaction** |

Purpose of this procedure

Customers (internal and external) have a great impact on work groups. They are the ones who set the requirements for a work group's products and services. This procedure will allow you to determine what the customers require of the work group and their level of satisfaction with the work group's products or services.

When to use this procedure

Use this procedure after you have negotiated the design project's purpose and scope and determined who the work group's customers are.

Before you start

1. Retrieve and review the descriptions from your preliminary assessment that identified

   - The work group's product or service outputs

   - Customers of the products or services

   - Customer requirements and satisfaction level with these products or services

   - The importance of these products or services to the organization's overall business strategy

   - Existing goals or objectives for these products and services

2. Highlight the information that's relevant to the work processes selected by the work group manager and members as the focus of the design project.

3. Ensure work group members receive general training in the concepts discussed in Section One of this book and in how the design process works and their roles in it. Training should include

   - The concepts and principles of whole systems

   - Principles of process, work group, and job design

   - Analysis tools and procedures

   - Design options and choices

   - Management and group expectations of how the group will

     — Plan

     — Solve problems

     — Make decisions

     — Give and receive feedback

     — Handle conflict

4. Develop a timetable to complete the procedure.

What to do

Steps	Specifics
1. Review with the work group your preliminary assessment findings about the work processes selected for this project.	Ask the group if there are any significant changes to make to the findings.
2. Assign structured customer interviews for each member of the work group.	Ask the group to draft interview questions to determine if the existing descriptions of customer requirements and levels of satisfaction are accurate.
3. Review customer answers with the work group.	Ask the group to indicate their confidence level in regard to the answers.
4. If the group indicates low confidence that customer answers are representative of the entire customer population, survey a representative sample of customers on the same subjects.	
5. Revise descriptions of customer requirements and satisfaction levels from the preliminary assessment.	Ask the group to reflect what they learned in the interviews and surveys in the revised descriptions.
6. Confirm that the work group's new descriptions coincide with its manager's understanding and with the strategic plans of the organization.	Ask the manager to • Confirm descriptions of relevant goals and objectives by comparing them to his or her plans for the work group. • Compare the group's actual performance (from performance records) to the manager's plans. List differences between the two. • Talk informally to the managers who drafted the organization's strategic plans.

Exhibit 3.1 shows a flowchart of this procedure.

Exhibit 3.1 Determining Customer Satisfaction

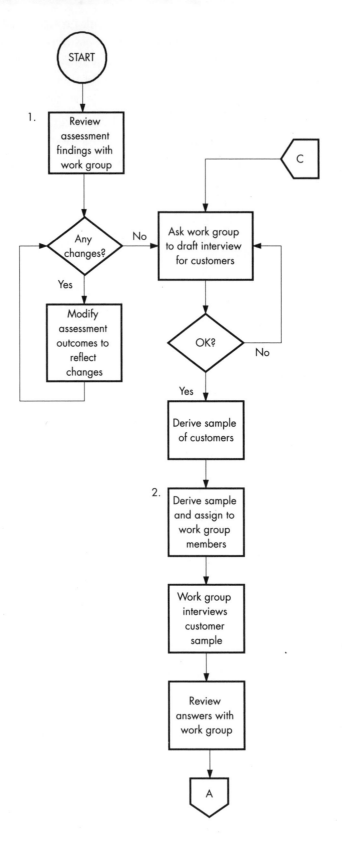

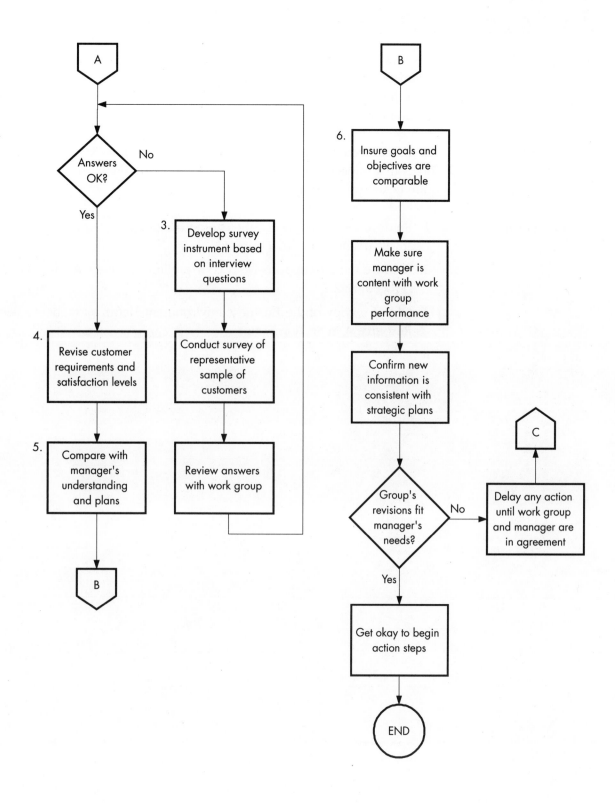

A

Answers OK? No

Yes

3. Develop survey instrument based on interview questions

4. Revise customer requirements and satisfaction levels

Conduct survey of representative sample of customers

5. Compare with manager's understanding and plans

Review answers with work group

B

B

6. Insure goals and objectives are comparable

Make sure manager is content with work group performance

Confirm new information is consistent with strategic plans

Group's revisions fit manager's needs? No Delay any action until work group and manager are in agreement C

Yes

Get okay to begin action steps

END

Set Goals and Objectives for Work Processes by Analyzing the Business Environment

Purpose of this procedure

This procedure has you analyze the external business environment to determine just how much external groups or forces impact the work group. From that data, the work group will be able to set goals and objectives for future interactions with those groups or forces.

When to use this procedure

Use this procedure after you have identified all of the external groups or forces that impact the work group and determined what those forces require of the work group.

Before you start

1. Retrieve the descriptions of customer requirements and satisfaction levels obtained in Procedure 3.1.

2. Retrieve the descriptions from your preliminary assessment (Procedure 2.2).

3. Obtain a copy of the Business Environment Matrix worksheet. (See Resource A in Section Four.)

Steps	Specifics
1. Conduct a meeting with the group manager and members.	
2. Have them share their confirmations or revisions of relevant information from the preliminary assessment.	Ask all participants to point out any "ahas" that the confirmation process revealed.
3. Estimate the impact of outside groups or forces on the work processes you're analyzing.	Copy the "Business Environment Matrix" onto a flip chart. (See Resource A in Section Four). Facilitate the group in completing the matrix.
4. Determine how well the current strategy and goals fit with anticipated changes in the environment.	Facilitate discussion and record answers.
5. Determine if the work group is flexible enough to deal with the anticipated rate of change in the environment.	Facilitate discussion and record answers.
6. Determine how well the goals and objectives of the immediate work group fit with the business strategy and the goals and objectives of the division (or other superordinate unit) to which the work group contributes.	Facilitate discussion and record answers.
7. List and reach a consensus on necessary changes to goals and objectives for the selected work processes.	Ask the group to revise its goals and objectives.

Exhibit 3.2 shows a sample of a partially completed business environment matrix (for a cabinet-making company, which will be used in various subsequent exhibits to illustrate procedures).

Exhibit 3.2 Business Environment Matrix

External Group/Force	What They Expect	What They Provide	Goals (Current and Future)
1. Customers	• Delivery on time • Quality crafting • Fair price • Durable, good-looking products	• Specs • Place and time for delivery	Maintain and increase quality levels
2. Materials suppliers (lumber and finishes)	• Orders on a regular basis • Prompt payment (within 60 days)	• Two-week delivery • High-quality materials • Fair financial arrangements	Reduce delays in delivery to 48 hours
3. Hardware and tool services			

CHAPTER 4

Technical Process Analysis: Understanding How the Group Creates Its Products and Services

Better results almost always require a better technical process. You'll remember from the introduction to this section that the technical process includes the

- Work flow

- Information flow

- Product or service requirements and the deficiencies resulting from them

The key to quality improvement, responsiveness, and reduced cycle time is managing this process. Process management involves finding the most direct path from customer need to a need-satisfying product or service. As organizations become more and more bureaucratic, they tend to evolve less and less direct paths. To find a better path, it helps to see your starting point. The preliminary assessment gave you some initial (though soft) data. This analysis goes much further in discovering what process improvements will be most beneficial.

Purpose of this chapter

In this chapter, the work group will use various procedures to trace its current path and locate where problems occur. This chapter provides the tools and steps to answer key questions about the technical process:

- How well is the work process designed to accomplish the group's goals and desired outcomes?

- How well does the arrangement of work space support the physical work flow?

- How well does the information flow support the work group in performing their tasks in an informed and timely manner?

How is this chapter organized?

To perform these activities:	Follow this procedure:
Identify the work group's process of receiving inputs and creating outputs and the associated requirements.	Procedure 4.1 — Determine Process Inputs and Outputs, Their Requirements, and Process Boundaries and Flow
Analyze when and where the work flow of the group crosses into other work groups.	Procedure 4.2 — Create a Relationship Map
Analyze when, where, and what types of information flow through the process.	Procedure 4.3 — Determine the Flow of Information through the Process
Determine how the work is done in relationship to the physical environment.	Procedure 4.4 — Identify Work Flow over the Physical Space
• Analyze the things that make up a product's or service's cycle time. • Spot non–value adding activities and delays.	Procedure 4.5 — Complete a cycle time analysis
• Give the entire work group an opportunity to provide input into the descriptions from the first five procedures. • Secure a group consensus about the work process.	Procedure 4.6 — Review and Revise First-Draft Process Descriptions
• Give the entire work group an opportunity to identify and describe process-related problems and root causes.	Procedure 4.7 — Find the Problems with the Current Technical Process

Meetings

Technical analysis should be conducted as efficiently as possible. Therefore, you should start with small group meetings with experienced members to draft the preliminary work. Then you can guide the entire group in reviewing and revising it. In addition, it's essential that you involve the entire group in finding problems in the current work and information flow. (If you tried to do this in small groups, you'd end up with scapegoating, and little agreement on problem definitions.)

Consequently, the technical analysis should involve two sets of meetings with both the small group and the large group. The table below explains their sequence and purpose.

Meetings of:	In this sequence:	Will focus on:
Small group	First set	• Establishing process inputs, outputs, boundaries, and requirements • Flowcharting process steps • Creating a relationship map • Mapping the information flow • Mapping the physical structures surrounding the work flow
	Second set	Completing the cycle time analysis
Entire work group	First set	Reviewing and revising first-draft descriptions
	Second set	Finding problems with the current technical process

Each set can consist of one or several meetings depending on the

- Amount of time participants can devote to each meeting
- Complexity of the process
- Extent of experience the members have
- Extent to which they agree about how work gets done

Tools to analyze the technical process

To gather information about the work flow, information flow, and process deficiencies, again you will use structured interviews. In addition, the following tools will be useful.

To analyze:	Use this tool:
Work flow	**Work-flow chart.** A diagram of the major steps that it takes to produce a product or service.
	Relationship map. A stratified flowchart. It shows when the work process crosses departmental or work group boundaries. (Each row of the chart represents a department involved in producing the end product or service. Diagram the work flow so that each action appears in the row of the department that performs it.) This tool makes it easy to spot convoluted work flows.
	Cycle time analysis worksheet. A worksheet on which you list
	• Major steps or events of a work process, including delays
	• The type of activity that each step or event entails, such as operations, transportation, storage, and inspection.
	• The amount of time each step or event typically takes
	This tool shows how much time the work process spends on non–value adding steps or events. (See the instructions and worksheet in Section Four, Resource B.)
	Work space map. A diagram of the work area with the work flow mapped out over the physical space. This tool makes it easy to spot physical barriers to the work flow.

To analyze:	Use this tool:

Information flow

Information-flow chart. A diagram of the flow of information across the work process. When you compare work flow to information flow, you can find information gaps (places where someone must make decisions about work without relevant information).

Specifications for:

• Products

List of state-changes. To produce a product, workers change raw materials into finished goods. Whenever materials change into a more-complete state, a state-change occurs. (For example, training materials typically include the following state-changes: from analysis documents to training outline to first-draft materials to finished deliverables.)

• Services

List of key decisions or interactions. To produce a service, workers notice indications of need and create corresponding services. In the process, key decisions or interactions occur (rather than state-changes).

Wherever a state-change or key decision or interaction occurs, specifications can be set. The work group can measure the product or service against these specifications to tell whether it is still in line with customer requirements.

(continued on next page)

To analyze:	Use this tool:

Departures from specifications

Product/service records. These indicate how well inputs and outputs meet standards and customer requirements.

Variance analysis worksheet. A variance is a defect, a place where a measurable output fails to meet standards. A variance analysis worksheet is a matrix for organizing critical information, including

- Cause of the variance
- Where it's found
- How it's fixed
- Who controls its occurrence

(See the Variance Analysis Worksheet in Section Four, Resource C. For more information, see Miller, 1991.)

Results

After analyzing the technical process, the group will reach agreement on

- The barriers and bottlenecks in the work process that keep the group from meeting its goals effectively and efficiently
- The best way to arrange work space in support of the work flow
- The information and the time needed to perform work and make decisions.

Once the group finds what's wrong with the technical process, it's ready to examine human structures and systems. A faulty technical process almost always creates conflict, and conflict often creates problems with the group's structures. Consequently, by finding problems with the technical process, the group can locate potential "hot spots" in its human structures and systems.

For More Information

Chang, R.Y. "Continuous Process Improvement." *Info-Line* (published by the American Society of Training and Development, October 1992). Explains the tools and steps of process analysis.

Galbraith, J. R. *Organization Design* (Reading, Mass.: Addison-Wesley, 1977), pp. 174–184. Describes how to select coordination mechanisms based on the information-processing requirements of the task.

Goal/QPC. *The Memory Jogger: A Pocket Guide of Tools for Continuous Improvement* (Methuen, Mass., 1988). Explains the tools and steps of process analysis.

Hackman, J. R. and Oldham, G. R. *Work Redesign* (Reading, Mass.: Addison-Wesley, 1980). Chapter 4, "Motivation through the Design of Work," describes principles of job design (pp. 71–98). Chapter 5, "Diagnosing Work Systems," describes how to assess existing jobs and provides norms for the Job Diagnostic Survey (pp. 99–129).

Hammer, M. and Champy, J. *Reengineering the Corporation* (New York: Harper Business, 1993). Chapter 3, "Rethinking Business Processes," describes principles of process design (pp. 50–64). Chapter 4, "The New World of Work," describes principles of work design (pp. 65–82).

Hanna, D. P. *Designing Organizations for High Performance* (Reading, Mass.: Addison-Wesley, 1988). Chapter 2, "An Organization Performance Model," and Chapter 3, "The Assessment Process," describe the assessment process (specifically, pp. 45–91).

Harbour, J. L. "Improving Work Processes." *Performance and Instruction,* February 1993, pp. 5–10. Provides principles of process design and explains how to analyze processes and cycle time.

Miller, L. M. *Designing for Total Quality* (Atlanta: Miller Consulting Group, 1991). Chapter 3, "Surveying the Environment" (pp. 61–86), and Chapter 5, "Technical Systems Design" (pp. 105–143), describe how to conduct business-environment and work-process analysis.

Miller, L. M. and Howard, J. *Managing Quality Through Teams* (Atlanta: Miller Consulting Group, 1991). Chapter 3, "Managing the Process," describes how to map out work flow, analyze cycle time, and identify critical information about variances (pp. 43–66). Chapter 9, "The Problem Solving Model," describes how to identify problems and find causes (pp. 145–159).

Rummler, G. A. and Brache, A. P. *Improving Performance* (San Fransisco: Jossey-Bass, 1990). Chapter 5, "The Process Level of Performance," describes how to map out work flow (pp. 44–63). Chapter 10, "Improving and Managing the Processes of the Organization," describes how to analyze processes (pp. 115–139).

Smith, P. and Kearny, L. *Creating Workplaces Where People Can Think* (San Francisco: Jossey-Bass, 1994). Presents detailed procedures for optimizing productivity and creativity through design of the physical workplace.

Determine Process Inputs and Outputs, Their Requirements, and Process Boundaries and Flow

Purpose of this procedure

Work groups follow a process (or processes) when making products or performing services. The process, depending on the product or service, can range from simple to complex. In all cases, work groups receive inputs to perform their required work. That work is then done within certain boundaries and according to some flow to create the final required output.

This procedure will allow you to determine the work group's process of receiving inputs and creating outputs and the associated requirements.

When to use this procedure

After you have analyzed the environment the work group operates within, the demands placed on it, and its goals, you're ready to map the processes the work group follows to meet its goals. In addition, whenever you want to check to make sure a new process is staying on track, or when the work group's context changes significantly, it can be helpful to remap the work process.

Before you start

1. Confirm with the work group's manager which work processes to analyze. Since process mapping can be tedious, ask the manager to select the highest-priority process to begin with. That process should

   - Have the greatest impact on external customer satisfaction

   - Provide the best balance of potential payoff to probable success. The more you change the current system, the *higher* the potential payoff, but the *lower* the probability of success.

2. Negotiate for half-day sessions, at a minimum, in which to do this work. The most efficient way to structure the nitty-gritty, first-draft work of process mapping is to conduct small group meetings with one or two experienced work group members. It's not efficient to do this kind of detailed work with the group as a whole. Gain commitment from the selected participants to complete all first-draft activities.

3. Inform participants ahead of time of the focus of the meeting: establishing process inputs, outputs, boundaries, and requirements, and flowcharting process steps.

4. Distribute a list of the principles of process design (from Section One) to the entire work group. Ask them to review and highlight principles that seem to be missing or violated by their existing technical process. Ask them to bring their highlighted list to the problem-finding meetings for the entire work group.

5. Develop a timetable to complete the procedure.

What to do

Steps	Specifics
1. Conduct a meeting with one or two of the most experienced members of the work group.	Record answers for the questions below.
2. Determine process **outputs.**	• What does the work group produce (or what services does the group provide)?
3. Determine process **boundaries.**	• Where does the work process begin and end?
4. Determine process **inputs.**	• What inputs does the work process begin with?
5. Determine process **interim outputs.**	• If you traced the creation of a specific product (or service) from beginning to end, what parts, things, or decisions do group members produce along the way?
6. Determine process **output requirements.**	• What purposes must the group's product (or service) fulfill? • To meet customer expectations and product (or service) specifications or standards, what criteria must the ultimate product or service meet?
7. Determine process **input requirements.**	• To meet work group expectations and input specifications, what criteria must the inputs meet?
8. Determine **interim output requirements.**	• To meet work group expectations and produce a final product (or service) that meets its associated requirements and specifications, what criteria must be met by the parts, things, or decisions produced along the way?

(continued on next page)

9. Given the above data and the knowledge of the participants, flowchart all the steps used to produce the selected process's end product (or service).

To allow you to add and delete steps as needed, write the steps on large self-stick notes, one to a note, and arrange them in sequence on a wall or other large blank surface.

At the beginning of the flowchart, place a box that lists process inputs. (If the inputs come from separate sources, use separate input boxes for each.)

At the end of the flowchart, place a box that lists the end product or service. (If there are multiple products or services, use separate output boxes for each.)

Between the beginning and the end of the flowchart, place boxes listing the major steps of the work process, one to a box. (It is valuable to add things such as the time needed to perform each step.)

10. Document the flowchart for future reference.

Save the flowchart as is, if possible. (You will need to use the self-stick notes on the flowchart in Procedure 4.2.) You might also have someone copy it onto smaller paper or enter it into a computer for future reference.

One person should be assigned to maintain all documentation from the analysis phase.

Exhibit 4.1 shows the types of information that might be obtained using this procedure, and Exhibit 4.1.1 shows a partially completed flowchart that might result from this procedure.

Exhibit 4.1 Desired Outcomes Worksheet

Steps	Activity	Specifics/Outcomes
1	Convene meeting with most experienced work group members.	An agenda that lists outcomes for the meeting: • Current process outputs. • Process boundaries. • Process inputs. • Interim outputs. • Output requirements. • Input requirements. • Interim output requirements. • Flowchart of overall process.
2	Determine process outputs.	List of the things and services the group produces, along with associated intrinsic results such as customer satisfaction and product loyalty.
3	Determine process boundaries.	The final action and event (performed by people outside the work group) before the work group can begin its work. The final action and event the work group performs before the output leaves the workplace.
4	Determine process inputs.	List of resources and things needed to perform the work, including materials, equipment, facility, and special circumstances, such as sterile conditions.
5	Determine interim process outputs.	List of artifacts and conditions that mark (serve to document) the events of the process. In effect, the results of each action taken by the work group.
6	Determine process output requirements.	List of the environmental, social, and economic wants of the customers. Customer expectations of all sorts, both experiential and health- and safety-related. Internal specifications for the product (or service).
7	Determine process input requirements.	Specification of the expectations of the work group as customers of those who supply inputs.
8	Determine interim output requirements.	List of criteria to be met by parts, things, or decisions produced along the way to meet work group expectations and produce a final product (or service) that satisfies its associated requirements and specifications.
9	Flowchart the process.	A visual representation of the inputs, process (with interim outputs), and outputs of the process.
10	Document the flowchart for future reference.	Flowchart in a format and style both the work group members and management will find easy to interpret and use.

Let's use a simple example to illustrate this idea and those to follow. Suppose a small cabinetmaking company has been commissioned by a large law firm to build custom-made bookcases for the firm's law library. The job is much larger than anything the company has ever done before. It doesn't require new equipment, skills, or procedures. However, the work is being done for a specified price, not to be exceeded, and there is a penalty clause if the bookcases are delivered late. The company can't afford to waste time or resources. If it does, it stands to lose a substantial sum and will probably go bankrupt. They have to do the job right the first time and they have to deliver the bookcases on time. If they are successful, they will make a very nice profit.

The key for the cabinetmakers is to make the best possible use of their technical process. So let's analyze their technical process. Understand we are thinking of the cabinetmakers as a single work group. In fact, in small cabinet shops, not only are the workers a single group, they are cross-trained so each worker can do any job that needs to be done.

Work flow

Exhibit 4.1.1 shows how the cabinetmakers make cabinets. Its purpose is to quickly provide an overall (big-picture) view of the operation.

The details will come out as we continue to investigate this little operation.

A caveat is needed at this point: no one has said they (the cabinetmakers) should change the way they do things.

Exhibit 4.1.1 Work-Flow Chart

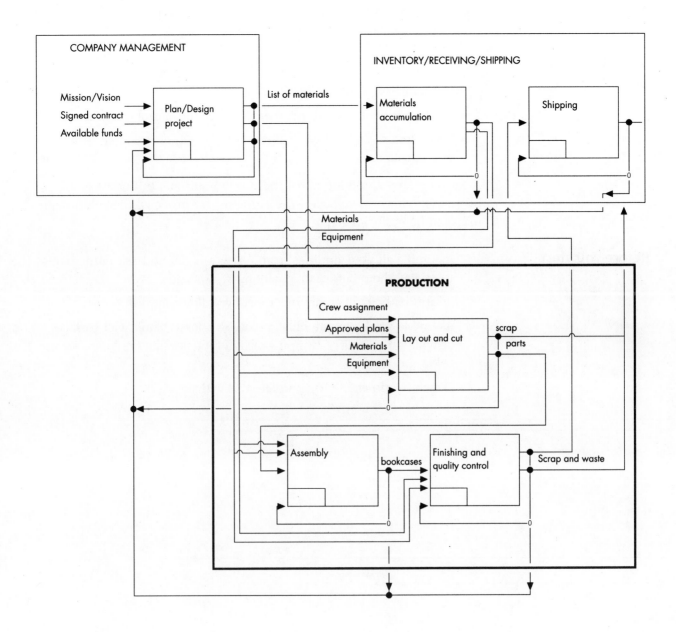

| Procedure 4.2 | **Create a Relationship Map** |

Purpose of this procedure

By visually depicting the process, the relationship map will provide greater understanding and help pinpoint process steps where change will be most beneficial.

When to use this procedure

Use this procedure when you need to determine

- If the process is convoluted
- How logically the work process flows in and out of other groups
- When and where the work flow of the group crosses into other work groups

After you have identified all of the inputs, outputs, boundaries, and requirements and flowcharted the steps in the process, the relationship map can be easily created.

Before you start

1. Assemble all your findings from Procedure 4.1 and ask participants to review them before this meeting.

2. Inform participants what this meeting will accomplish.

3. Assemble working materials, including a large blank wall surface or whiteboard, self-stick notes of different sizes and colors, and colored markers.

4. Develop a timetable to complete this activity.

What to do

Steps	Specifics
1. Create a relationship map template.	Draw horizontal rows or bands across the length of the surface and add a vertical line along the left side to use as a column to list the other departments or groups involved in your work group's process.
2. Label the map.	At the top of the map, above the rows, list the process name.
	Using self-stick notes, in the left column and starting at the top row, label the name(s) of the department(s) and group(s) that provide the inputs into your work group's process.
	Label each row with the names of all the other departments or work groups involved in the process, one name per row. (Use the process flowchart from Procedure 4.1 to place these groups in the relative order, top-down, in which they are involved in the process.)
	Label the last row with the department or group receiving your group's output (the customer of the final product or service).
3. Re-create the work-flow chart from Procedure 4.1.	Transfer the self-stick notes from the work-flow chart to the relationship map, placing the notes in the proper row depending on the department or group responsible for the step.
	Make sure the work flow follows the same sequence on the new map.
	Add any additional details (time, tools, equipment, etc.) not found on the work-flow chart labels.

(continued on next page)

Steps	Specifics
4. Review the relationship map for completeness.	Ask these questions: • Is *anything* missing from the work process steps? • Are any other work groups or departments involved?
5. Document the completed map for reference in later stages of analysis and in the design process.	An exact copy of the map should be written on paper or entered into a computer. The map should be given to the individual responsible for maintaining documentation.

Exhibit 4.2 shows an example of a partially completed relationship map.

Exhibit 4.2 Relationship Map

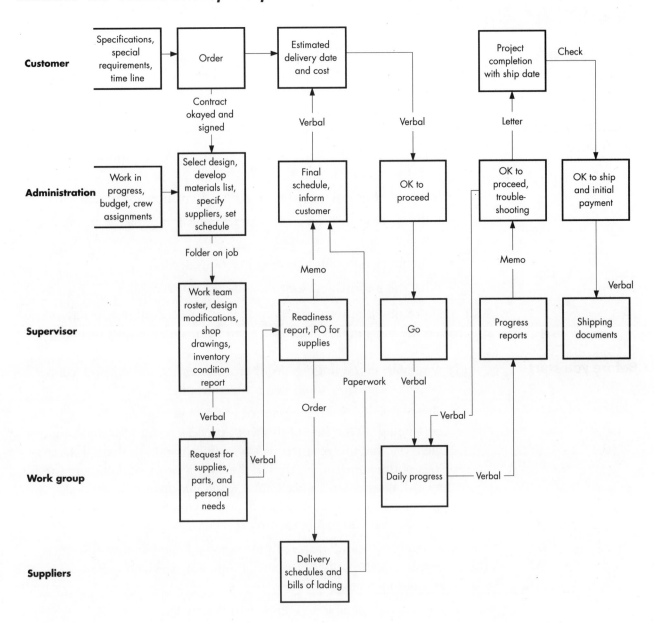

Procedure 4.3	## Determine the Flow of Information Through the Process

Purpose of this procedure

As with the work-flow chart and relationship map, by visually portraying the information flow, you will gain a greater understanding of the role information plays and how greatly it impacts the work process.

When to use this procedure

Use this procedure when you need to know

- When, where, and what types of information flow through the process
- If the work group receives the right information at the right time
- If the work group can easily extract critical information from all it receives
- If incoming and outgoing information is accurate
- What the information sources and destinations are

It is more efficient to chart the information flow after you have flow-charted the steps in the work process *and* created the relationship map.

Before you start

1. Assemble all the findings from Procedures 4.1 and 4.2 and ask participants to review them before this meeting.

2. Give participants advance notice of this meeting (two to four weeks, depending on the size of the work process being analyzed). Inform them of what this meeting will accomplish and ask them to keep logs of the information used in their work process. Ask them to record information sources, time when information is needed, amounts of information needed, and anything else information-specific that you feel is relevant to this work group.

3. Assemble working materials, including a large blank wall surface or whiteboard, self-stick notes of different sizes and colors, and colored markers.

4. Develop a timetable to complete this activity.

What to do

Steps	Specifics
1. Post large copies of the work-flow chart and relationship map on the wall.	
2. Identify **where** information is needed to make decisions.	For both the relationship map and work-flow chart, ask participants to write the locations where decisions are made on one color of self-stick note.
	On a three-point scale ranging from major decision to minor decision, ask them to also rate each of those decisions by placing a number on its self-stick note.
	Place each note on its appropriate location on each chart.
3. Identify **what** information is needed to make the decisions or perform the work.	Using a different color self-stick note, ask participants to identify where such things as plans, reports, standards or specifications, and other documents are used in the process.
	Place each note on its relative location on each chart.
4. Document these findings for reference in later stages of analysis and in the design process.	The completed posters should be given to the individual responsible for maintaining documentation.

Exhibit 4.3 shows an example of a partially completed information-flow chart.

Exhibit 4.3   Information-Flow Chart

The flow of information for our cabinetmakers is much simpler than for other kinds of operations. But it illustrates well the basic patterns that exist in most organizations.

The only dialogue situation between the work group and management occurs in the first phase of construction, where special problems might occur. Once the work is progressing "normally," information is processed by management and decisions are made before the work group is informed or given a chance to provide further input.

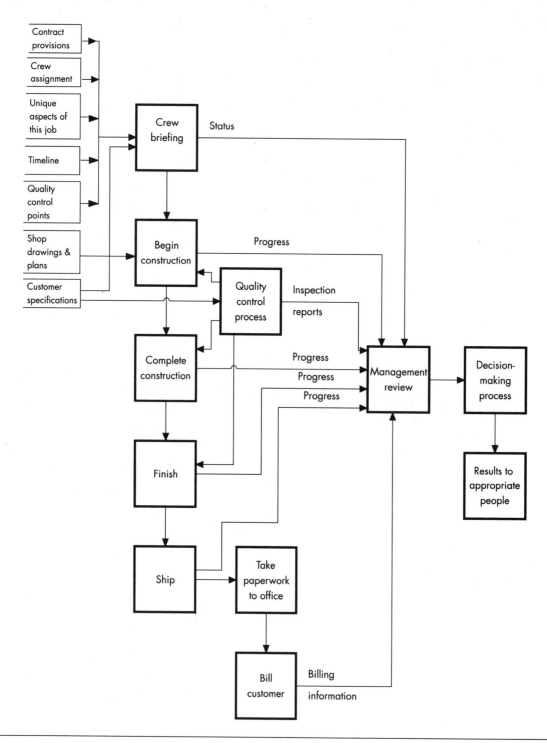

Identify Work Flow over the Physical Space

Purpose of this procedure

Mapping the flow of work over the physical space provides additional insight into ways to improve the work process. By analyzing how the work is done in relationship to the environment where it is done, you will be able to determine if the work space is best suited to the work process.

When to use this procedure

This procedure is most useful when previous analyses show the work is accomplished in a large physical setting or flows through numerous settings.

Before you start

1. You may find it useful to read Smith and Kearny's *Creating Workplaces Where People Can Think* (1994).

2. Obtain a copy of the floor plan(s) of the space where the work occurs.

3. Distribute copies of the floor plan(s) to participants before the meeting. Ask them to trace the work flow, as they see it, on their copies. Retrieve the completed floor plans before the meeting.

4. Observe the work group and trace the work flow on a copy of the floor plan(s).

5. Diagram each person's rendition of the physical work flow on a master copy of the floor plan(s). Use a different color for each person's version. Enlarge this copy to post on a wall.

6. Develop a timetable to complete this activity.

What to do

Steps	Specifics
1. Post the copy of the master floor plan on a wall.	
2. Point out any significant differences between each person's rendition of the work flow.	Ask the participants to reach a consensus on the work flow through the physical space.
3. Document these findings for reference in later stages of analysis and in the design process.	The completed floor plan(s) should be given to the individual responsible for maintaining documentation.

Exhibit 4.4 shows a sample floor plan of a work space, and Exhibit 4.4.1 shows an example of a partially completed physical work flow.

Exhibit 4.4   Floor Plan

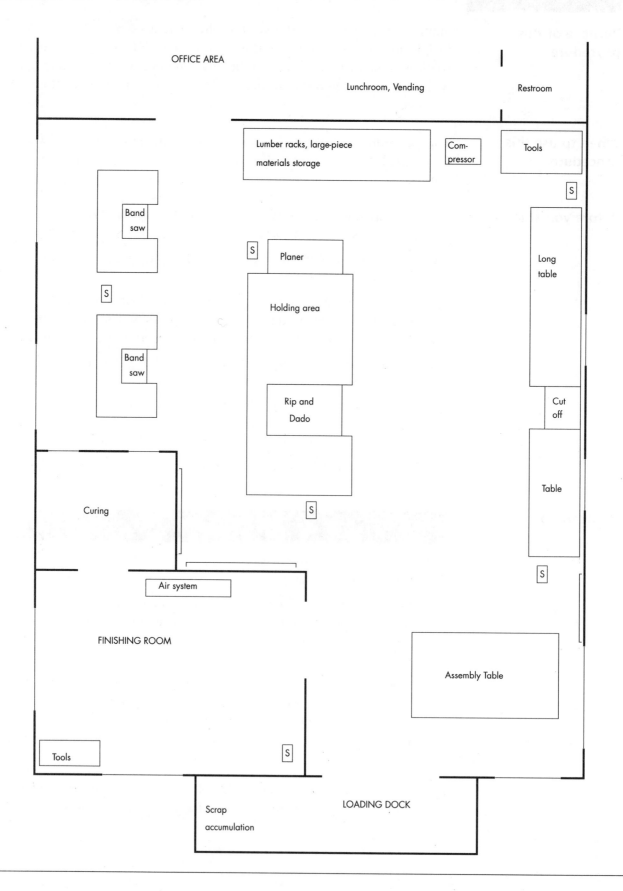

OFFICE AREA

Lunchroom, Vending

Restroom

Lumber racks, large-piece materials storage

Com-
pressor

Tools

S

Band
saw

Long
table

S

S

Planer

Holding area

Band
saw

Cut
off

Rip and
Dado

Table

S

Curing

S

Air system

FINISHING ROOM

Assembly Table

Tools

S

Scrap
accumulation

LOADING DOCK

Exhibit 4.4.1   Physical Work Flow Diagram

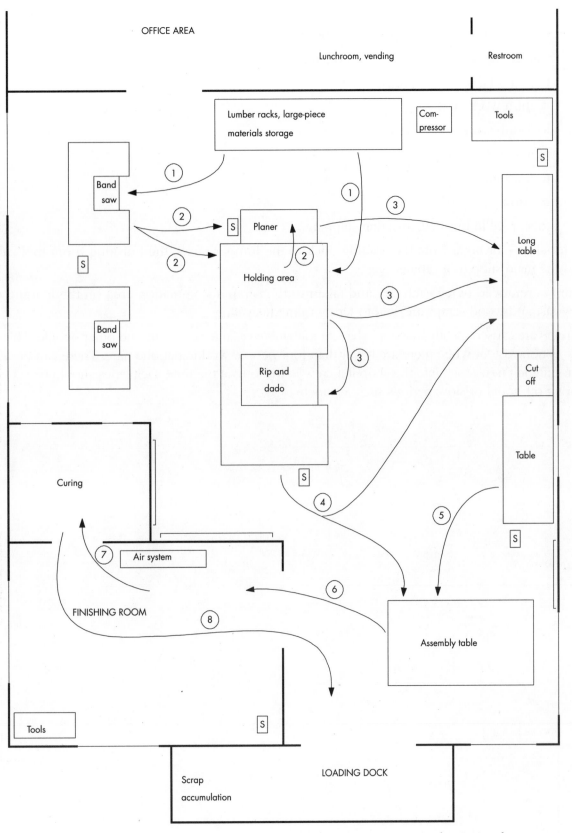

(continued on next page)

Exhibit 4.1.1 *(cont)*

Work flow is indicated by the circled numbers:

1. From storage to first work area or holding...

2. ...to second area or holding

3. ...to third work area

4. ...to fourth work area or assembly

5. ...to assembly

6. ...to finishing

7. ...to curing

8. ...to storage in finishing awaiting shipping.

Materials are brought from the loading dock to the lumber racks, the finishing room tool cabinet, and the main shop tool cabinet.

Scrap is removed twice each day and taken to the scrap accumulation area on the loading dock. Sawdust and wood scraps are sold to Jersey Clime Recycling.

Barriers are caused mostly by people having to maneuver large pieces around other people. This problem is nonexistent when there are fewer than four people working at one time. There can be a problem bringing new stock into the shop if a crew is working at the time. Deliveries should be scheduled during off hours or slow periods such as lunch.

Complete a Cycle Time Analysis

Purpose of this procedure

This procedure allows you to analyze the things that make up a product's or service's cycle time. This allows you to spot non–value adding activities and delays. To improve cycle time, the new process will eliminate or reduce these things.

When to use this procedure

This is a critical procedure in work process design. All findings up to this point will provide input into the cycle time analysis.

Before you start

1. Schedule a meeting involving one or two experienced work group members.

2. Give participants copies of the results from Procedures 4.1–4.4 to review before the meeting.

3. Make a copy of the Cycle Time Analysis Worksheet. (See Resource B in Section Four.)

4. Develop a timetable to complete this activity.

What to do

Steps	Specifics
1. Post copies of the work-flow chart and relationship map on a wall.	Tell the participants to refer to these throughout the meeting.
2. Following the directions to complete the Cycle Time Analysis Worksheet. (See Resource B in Section Four.)	Ask the participants to reach a consensus on all the activities listed, the categories selected, and the time noted.
3. Perform these calculations.	<ul><li>The total amount of time it takes to produce the product or service.</li><li>The amount of time the product or service spends in value-adding activity (such as "Operations").</li><li>The amount of time the product or service spends in non–value adding activities (such as "Transportation," "Storage," "Inspection," and "Delay").</li><li>The percentage of the total time that the product or service spends in non–value adding activity.</li></ul>

Exhibit 4.5 shows an example of a partially completed Cycle Time Analysis Worksheet.

Exhibit 4.5 Cycle Time Analysis (Cabinetmaking Company)

Activity	Activity Type	Time Spent
Brief work team about the project and critical aspects	O	15 min
Set up equipment	T	90 min
Set materials movement patterns through working area and scrap movement away from working area	O	20 min
Design and develop templates for 4 x 8 stock	O	75 min
Train bandsaw operators	D	30 min
END PREPARATORY STEPS	—	—
Lay out template on stock	O	10 min
Cut stock (per bookcase)	O	30 min
Inspect cut	I	5 min
Allow for rework	R	20 min
Rough-in joints	O	30 min
Sand	O	10 min
Apply prefinish	O	10 min
Inspect	I	5 min
Allow for rework	R	20 min
Wait for oil to penetrate	D	15 min
END LAY-OUT AND CUT	—	—
Preassemble and complete jointing	O	30 min
QA inspection	I	5 min
Glue, clamp and fasten	O	15 min
Clean glue, etc. from piece	O	5 min
QA inspection	I	5 min
Fine sand and buff	O	25 min
Clean work area	D	15 min
END ASSEMBLY	—	—
Prime	O	5 min
Apply first coat lacquer and buff	O	15 min
Wait for tack	D	30 min
Apply second through fourth coats	O	30 min
Wait for tack	D	90 min

(continued on next page)

Exhibit 4.5 Cycle Time Analysis (Cabinetmaking Company) *(cont)*

Activity	Activity Type	Time Spent
Buff with lambswool	O	30 min
QA inspection	I	5 min
Apply final coat	O	10 min
Wait for hard gloss	D	90 min
Final buff	O	10 min
END FINISHING	—	—
Cure	S	N/A
Final inspection	I	20 min
Move to shipping	T	15 min

Review and Revise First-Draft Process Descriptions

Purpose of this procedure

This procedure gives the entire work group an opportunity to provide input into the descriptions from the first five procedures. This will also allow you to get group consensus about the work process.

When to use this procedure

This step should immediately follow the small group meetings with the experienced group members.

Before you start

1. Schedule a meeting involving the entire work group.

2. Give participants copies of the results from Procedures 4.1–4.5 to review before the meeting.

3. Develop a timetable to complete this activity.

What to do

Steps	Specifics
1. Post copies of the work-flow chart, relationship map, information-flow chart, and physical work flow diagram.	Tell participants they will refer to these throughout the meeting.
2. Review the process's boundaries, inputs, outputs, and requirements.	Ask if there are any general questions or concerns.
2. Facilitate the group in reaching consensus on these things.	If the work group *cannot* reach consensus on customer requirements, it's a good idea to have them observe customers using the product.
3. Have one of the members who participated in the flowcharting explain the • Work-flow chart • Relationship map • Information-flow chart • Physical work flow	Ask for general questions or concerns.
4. Facilitate the group in reaching consensus on the steps and flow of each of these.	If the group cannot reach consensus on these things and time permits, have the group select two members to observe the work process in action. Have them pay careful attention to state changes in the process. This allows them to see overlooked steps or delays.

<table>
<tr><td>**Procedure 4.7**</td><td></td></tr>
</table>

Find the Problems with the Current Technical Process

Purpose of this procedure

This procedure gives the entire work group an opportunity to identify and describe process-related problems and root causes. It is *not* intended to place blame on others.

When to use this procedure

This set of meetings should closely follow the Procedure 4.6 meeting, when information is fresh in the work group members' minds. Allow a day or two to pass between the two meetings, however, to allow the group members to absorb and assimilate the information.

Before you start

1. Schedule a meeting involving the entire work group.

2. Give participants a list of the principles of process design and ask them to highlight those principles that seem to be missing or violated in their current work process.

3. Develop a timetable to complete this activity.

What to do

Steps	Specifics
1. Post copies of the work-flow chart, relationship map, information-flow chart, and physical work flow diagram on a wall.	Tell participants they will refer to these throughout the meeting.
2. Discuss the principles that group members found to be missing or violated in the current work process.	Make sure the focus of the discussion is on process design. Be sure to keep the group focused on describing problems and finding root causes, *not* on finding "guilty parties." Keep reminding them that the more they blame rather than describe, the more likely critical information will be withheld and their time wasted.

Steps	Specifics
3. Locate mismatches between process and group boundaries.	On the relationship map, highlight places where the work process crosses boundaries from the work group to other departments. Ask how to control the quality, quantity, consistency, and time-liness of the process's outputs: • What additional major steps in the work flow could be included within this work group's boundaries? • What things does this work group currently do that do not contribute to its products or services?
4. Facilitate the work group in completing a variance analy-sis worksheet. (See Resource C in Section Four.)	Ask the group to think through the steps in the work process. At each step ask these questions: • What can go wrong? (This is the *cause* of the variance.) • What effect does this have on the output? (This is the *variance.*) • Where does the defect first get noticed? • Where does it typically get fixed? • Who controls whether or not the defect will occur?
5. Ask the group to examine the work flow (on the work-flow chart and relationship map).	Ask members to find and highlight: • Convoluted sequences (where the work flow takes a winding or indirect path). • Illogical, missing, or redundant steps.

(continued on next page)

Steps	Specifics
6. Ask the group to examine the cycle time analysis.	Ask members to find and highlight non–value adding activities such as inspection, transportation, storage, and delays.
7. Ask the group to examine the physical work flow diagram and notice how work moves across the work space.	Ask members to find and highlight barriers to the work flow.
8. Ask the group to examine the information-flow chart.	List the information needed to support each step in the work-flow chart (not the information-flow chart).
	Ask members to compare the two charts.
	Ask members to find and record places where work group members don't get the information they need. Look for problems such as:
	• Insufficient information
	• Unnecessary information
	• Confusing information
	• Indirect information (information that doesn't go *directly* to the member of the work group who is responsible for doing that step).

Steps	Specifics
9. Summarize and discuss.	Ask how well the work process is designed to accomplish the desired levels of • Quality • Quantity • Timeliness • Consistency • Flexibility • Customer satisfaction Ask how well the arrangement of work space supports the physical work flow. Ask how well the information flow supports the work group in performing their tasks in an informed and timely manner.
10. List and reach consensus on aspects of the technical process that need to change.	Prioritize problems by how much they: • Block the group from reaching its desired outcomes • Impact customer satisfaction • Are within the group's power (or the group's manager's power) to change

Exhibit 4.7 shows an example of a partially completed variance analysis worksheet.

Exhibit 4.7   Variance Analysis Worksheet

Variance	Cause	Where found?	How fixed?	Who controls its occurrence?
Saw travels more than 1/8 in. outside line on tight curves	Worker trying to saw too quickly	Band saw operations	Had to rework pieces	Individual worker
Sag in intermediate coat application	Spray nozzle releases too much lacquer	B & B cabinets	Had to refinish two cabinets	Supervisor (must set nozzle aperture)

CHAPTER 5

Human Systems Analysis: Understanding How People and Jobs Are Organized and Supported

In the previous chapter you identified problems with the technical process. However, even the most streamlined technical process cannot improve quality, responsiveness, and cycle time if it's based on top-down decision making and narrowly skilled jobs. In this chapter, the work group will analyze its human structures and support systems, including

- Structure, lines of authority, and coordination mechanisms — how people are organized, directed, and coordinated

- Job design — how work gets distributed into individual jobs

- Human resource systems — how people are selected, trained, evaluated, compensated, rewarded, and disciplined

- Values and norms — what gets rewarded (both formally and informally), as well as what people believe is important

Purpose of this chapter

Well-designed human structures and systems unite thinking and doing, engage work groups in goal setting and self-control, and are built on enriched, multiskilled jobs. In these procedures the work group will find out where their human structures and systems fail to support their desired outcomes. These procedures provide the tools and steps to answer key questions about human structures and systems:

- How well does the work group's structure support decision making nearest to the line of action?

- How effective is coordination of the group's work? Is work coordinated so that the group can make seamless and timely hand-offs?

- How effective are existing human resources systems (such as selection, training, and reward systems)? Do they support the level of ownership and teamwork necessary to reach the group's goals and achieve its quality of work life?

- How well do existing values and norms support the group's goals and desired outcomes?

How is this chapter organized?

Meetings

Like the technical process analysis, the human structure and support systems analysis requires a group effort. Therefore, for this analysis you will hold three group meetings. In addition, group members will perform individual assessments of job designs. The table below explains the sequence and purposes of these meetings.

Meetings of:	In this sequence:	Will focus on:
Current work group	First	Identifying those outside the group who might be affected by structural changes
Expanded group — both the original work group and those identified who might be affected by changes	Second	Analyzing structures and human systems
Individual assessments	Third	Individually examining job designs
Expanded group	Fourth	• Summarizing findings • Prioritizing problems

**Tools to analyze
the human structure
and support systems**

To gather information about the group's structure, job designs, values, and norms, again you will use structured interviews. In addition, the following tools will be useful.

To analyze:	Use this tool:
Organization of people	**Comparison of group boundaries to work process boundaries.** To determine how appropriately people are grouped, compare the steps that the work group does to the steps that their entire work process includes. The more steps that *other* groups do, the more inappropriate the grouping.
	Responsibility chart. A matrix (created by Beckhard and Harris [1987]) that lists • Work process steps or decisions • Names of contributors, including work group members, managers, and resource staff • Level of responsibility for each step or decision This tool makes it easy to spot divisions between responsibility and authority and between doing and decision making. (See the Responsibility Chart in Section Four, Resource D.)
Skill or incentive gaps in the current work group	**Skills and incentives matrix.** A matrix that identifies • Skills needed to do each step of a work process • The presence or absence of each skill in the current work group • The consequences (rewards and punishments) that influence the use of each skill (See the Skills and Incentives Matrix in Section Four, Resource E.)

To analyze:	Use this tool:
Degree to which jobs promote ownership and initiative	**Job diagnostic survey.** A survey that assesses how involving individual jobs are. It rates jobs on five dimensions:

   1. Skill variety — the variety of skills an employee uses on the job

   2. Task identity — the extent to which the job produces a "whole" identifiable output

   3. Task significance — the job's perceived importance

   4. Autonomy — the amount of discretion that the job allows an employee

   5. Intrinsic feedback — the extent to which the job itself provides indicators of how well the employee has done

(Based on a public-domain survey created by Hackman and Oldham [1980].)

Results

After analyzing the human structures and support systems, the work group will reach agreement on

- Who needs to be included in the ongoing process of job design
- What the group needs control over to provide its products or services
- Misalignments between the responsibility and authority levels of members
- Coordination problems in the process
- Skills and incentive deficits in the group
- Job design factors affecting the process
- The highest-impact problems to solve

For More Information

Beckhard, R. and Harris, R. T. *Organizational Transitions: Managing Complex Change* (Reading, Mass.: Addison-Wesley, 1987). Chapter 4, "The Change Process: Why Change?" describes how to define the importance and urgency of forces driving the change (pp. 29–44). Chapter 5, "Defining the Future State," describes how to identify the ultimate goal of change as well as midpoint goals (pp. 45–56). Chapter 6, "Assessing the Present," describes how to define the present state and determine readiness for change (pp. 57–70). Chapter 10, "Commitment Planning and Strategies," in the Responsibility Charting section, describes the responsibility-charting process you will use in this chapter (pp. 104–113).

Galbraith, J. R. *Organization Design* (Reading, Mass.: Addison-Wesley, 1977). Describes how to select coordination mechanisms based on the information-processing requirements of the task (pp. 174–184).

Hackman, J. R. and Oldham, G. R. *Work Redesign* (Reading, Mass.: Addison-Wesley, 1980). Chapter 4, "Motivation through the Design of Work," describes principles of job design (pp. 71–98). Chapter 5, "Diagnosing Work Systems," describes how to assess existing jobs and provides norms for the job diagnostic survey (pp. 99–129).

Hanna, D. P. *Designing Organizations for High Performance* (Reading, Mass.: Addison-Wesley, 1988). Chapter 2, "An Organization Performance Model," and Chapter 3, "The Assessment Process," describe the assessment process (specifically, pp. 45–91).

Lawler, E. E. *The Ultimate Advantage* (San Francisco: Jossey-Bass, 1992). Chapter 2, "Choosing the Right Management Style," explains how to select appropriate design components for the business strategy, environment, work process or technology, and labor force (pp. 25–48).

Lytle, W. O. *Socio-Technical Systems Analysis and Design Guide for Linear Work* (Plainfield, N.J.: Block Petrella Weisbord, 1991). Part 2, "Analysis of the Business Environment"; Part 3, "Technical System Analysis"; Part 4, "Social System Analysis"; and Part 5, "Summary of Analyses"; describe, in detail, how to complete this same kind of analysis for an entire business or business division (pp. 5–98).

Miller, L. M. and Howard, J. *Managing Quality Through Teams* (Atlanta: Miller Consulting Group, 1991). Chapter 3, "Managing the Process," describes how to map out work flow, analyze cycle time, and identify critical information about variances (pp. 43–66). Chapter 9, "The Problem Solving Model," describes how to identify problems and find causes (pp. 145–159).

Mohrman, S. A. and Cummings, T. G. *Self-Designing Organizations* (Reading, Mass.: Addison-Wesley, 1989). Chapter 6, "Diagnosing," describes how to identify gaps between the current and desired situation (pp. 67–84).

| Procedure 5.1 | ***Identify and Orient Outsiders Who Might Be Affected by Structural Change*** |

Purpose of this procedure

This procedure asks the current work group to identify those outside the work group who might be affected by changes to its work process, and the ways in which they might be affected. Those outsiders will then be oriented to the findings to date and asked to participate in future design work.

When to use this procedure

After the existing technical process has been analyzed, the work group can readily identify others who are involved in the work it does. Those other individuals need to be considered in any structural changes the work group plans on making if the new process is to function properly. Therefore, this procedure specifies who needs to be involved before proceeding in the design effort.

Before you start

1. Review the results of the technical process analysis. In the second meeting of the entire group, you compared the work process boundaries to the work group's boundaries. Did it look like the process depends on players from other departments? If so, the group's structure may need to change. It may need to propose one of the following structural changes:

   - Expand to include participants in the process that are currently outside the work group; these people would report to the work group's manager in either a direct-line or a dotted-line relationship. (A dotted-line relationship is one in which an employee is doing work for a manager who does *not* write his or her performance appraisal. The manager is *not* the employee's primary manager.)

   - Assign a process manager to oversee the entire process. This manager would establish each employee's contribution to the process. Functional managers (including the work group's manager) would evaluate individual performance by these measures.

   - Establish a matrix structure so that each person who works on the process reports both to a functional manager and to a process manager or team leader.

2. Distribute the findings from Procedure 4.7. Ask group members to review and make a list of individuals outside the work group who might be affected by structural changes to the process.

Steps	Specifics
1. Conduct a meeting with all members of the work group.	
2. Review mismatches between the work process and the group's boundaries.	Ensure that consensus remains about the problems identified in Procedure 4.7.
3. Have members share lists of outsiders who will be affected by changes to the process.	Create a master list of the individuals or groups identified.
4. Facilitate the group in reaching consensus about the impact of change on the outsiders.	Ask these questions: • How might each individual or group be affected? • What might be the impact on each person of each possible structural change? (Refer to the list on page 111.) • Record answers.
5. Brainstorm ways to get the constructive participation of those who might be affected.	Ask how best to involve the outsiders in • Briefings about the findings of the environmental and technical analyses • Analysis of the group's current structure • Design of a better system
6. Select and apply the strategies that will work best for each outsider affected.	
7. Hold briefings for those who may be affected to explain the design project's purpose, the findings to date, the potential impact of changes on them, and the potential benefits of participation.	You may hold either one-on-one or group briefings, depending on which format current work group members think will be more persuasive.

Exhibit 5.1 shows an example of the outputs of this procedure.

Exhibit 5.1 Outsider Identification and Orientation

This activity can be recorded in a number of ways. Normally each member of the group takes informal notes as the discussion progresses. These notes are then modified and added to during the meeting until finally they are gathered into some kind of summary document. The summary could be a matrix showing customers and other contacts in one column, the kinds and nature of the contacts in another, and the responses required by the work group in a third. For example:

Customer Service Contacts	Type and Nature	Response
Retailers	Customer complaints	Identify problem and troubleshoot
Distributors	Orders	Process, negotiate price, and verify

Such a matrix could show a great deal of detail. In most situations the more the work group can supply the better.

(continued on next page)

Exhibit 5.1 *(cont.)*

Another valuable expedient is to display the relationships in a simple diagram showing the nature and direction of information flow.

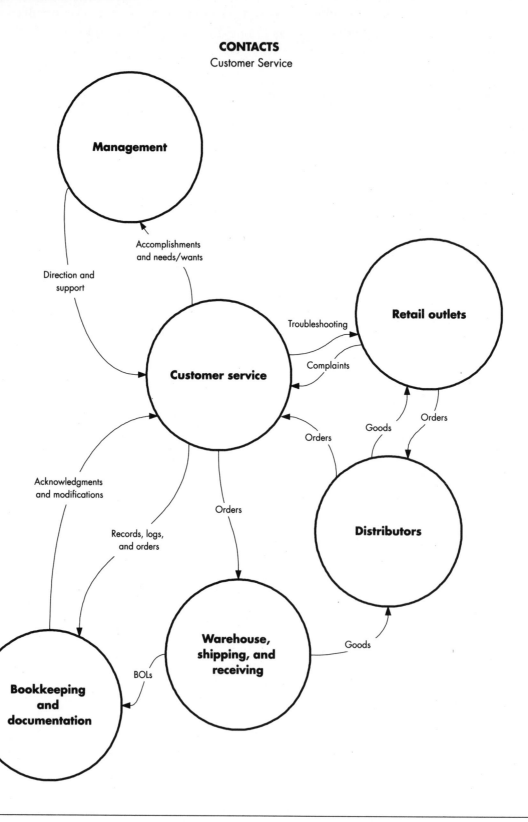

CONTACTS
Customer Service

Once the customer contacts have been displayed and agreed upon by the group, it can consider how changes might affect the relationships. For example, if the goal were to eliminate, as much as they could, the middleman from the customer service operation in these displays, the effects might include these:

Change	Customer(s) Affected	Consequences
Distributors direct order from warehouse	Distributors	1. Less paperwork 2. Faster response 3. Less hassle
	Warehouse	1. Requires better record keeping 2. Could cause resupply problem 3. Adds clerical staff at warehouse 4. Reduces staff in customer service
Retailers direct order from Customer Service	Management	1. Requires new marketing effort aimed at getting retailers to deal with parent company 2. Requires sales staff to service retailers directly 3. Requires added support and administration of new function 4. Involves added responsibilities for customer service, troubleshooting, order processing, etc. 5. Requires additional customer service staff and skills
	Retailers	1. Forces them to deal with new, unfamiliar sources 2. Reduces their cost 3. Will cause them to deal with higher volume per order
	Distributors	1. Loss of business 2. Forces them to turn to a competitor to supply equivalent goods

The group would then focus on the changes that affect them directly. For example, the Customer Service group would *not* work on consequences to management, but rather those they controlled directly, like troubleshooting retailer problems. They might bring in a select group of retail customers to brainstorm the consequences listed in the matrix.

It's important to document the results of these sessions and to begin implementation quickly so the external participants can get confirmation that their input is being seriously considered and used.

Analyze Structures and Human Resource Systems

Purpose of this procedure

This procedure will help the expanded group reach consensus on the following:

- What it needs to control to best produce its products or services
- Who has responsibilities throughout the work process
- Problems related to coordination and handoffs in the process
- Skill and incentive deficits in the group

These findings set the stage for prioritizing the problems that must be solved.

When to use this procedure

Your analysis of structures and human resources systems should follow your analyses of the environment and the technical process. That's because group boundaries and other individuals affected by the work process will have been identified. Those individuals can now be involved in the last steps of analysis, and throughout the design phase.

Before you start

1. Review the results of the technical analysis with the entire group.

2. Prepare copies of the completed relationship map and variance analysis worksheet from Chapter 4, Procedures 4.2 and 4.7.

3. Distribute to the entire work group a list of the principles of work group and job design. Ask them to read these principles and highlight principles that seem to be missing or violated in their existing work group and job composition. Ask them to bring their highlighted list to the problem-finding meetings for the entire work group.

4. Inform participants what this meeting will accomplish.

5. Assemble working materials, including a large blank surface (e.g., a large whiteboard or large flipchart) and colored markers.

6. Develop a timetable to complete this activity.

What to do

1. Review with newcomers the mismatches between process and group boundaries.

   On the relationship map developed during the technical process analysis, Procedure 4.7, highlight places where the work process crosses boundaries from the work group to other groups or departments.

2. Facilitate the group in reaching consensus about *what* the group needs to control to produce its products or services.

   Do *not* try to reach consensus, just yet, on *how* to add needed steps or skills. (You will discuss these things in the design stage.)

   Ask the group what it should add to control the quality, quantity, consistency, and timeliness of its products and services:

   - What additional steps in the work flow should the work group include?

   - What additional specialized skills does the group need to include?

   Ask the group what things it currently does that do *not* contribute to its products or services.

3. Facilitate the group in identifying who's responsible for each step in the work process and in finding mismatches between authority and responsibility.

   Complete a responsibility chart. (See instructions and worksheet in Section Four, Resource D.)

   Copy the chart onto the large working surface and then fill it in.

   Find problems with the existing distribution of responsibility and authority. Highlight:

   - Steps in which more than one person has responsibility.

   - Steps in which the person who is responsible for taking action does *not* have the authority to decide what to do.

   Record and maintain these findings.

   (continued on next page)

Steps	Specifics
4. Facilitate the group in finding any coordination problems. (Based on Jay Galbraith's [1977] guidelines, pp. 174–84.)	On the relationship map, locate the places where handoffs occur. List these places.
	Compare the above list to the variances listed on the variance analysis worksheet. List handoffs that seem related to variances. These are coordination problems.
	Categorize the type of coordination that occurs at each problem point as:
	• Rules and methods
	• Management decisions
	• Contact between managers whose areas are involved
	• Direct contact between "doers" in areas involved
	• Matrix work groups
	Highlight areas with complex or unpredictable coordination
5. Facilitate the group in finding any skill and incentive deficits.	Complete a skills and incentive matrix. (See instructions and worksheet in Section Four, Resource E.)
	Copy the matrix onto a large working surface and then fill it in.
	Ask the group to find skill deficits. Highlight missing skills.
	Sort missing skills into those for which adequate training, job aids, or apprenticeships are and are not available.
	Find incentive deficits. Highlight skills for which there is no reward *or* punishment.
	Sort skills with incentive deficits into skills for which incentives are and are not critical.

Exhibit 5.2 shows a sample of a partially completed responsibility chart for a customer service work group. Exhibit 5.2.1 shows an example of the types of weaknesses that can be found using the matrix.

Exhibit 5.2 Responsibility Chart

Overall Task	Performances	Person Responsible
Order processing	Taking order from distributor	Customer Service Representative (CSR)
	Transmitting order to Shipping	CSR
	Verifying order	Shipping
	Documentating the transaction	CSR and Shipping
	Informing distributor of ship date/time and ETA	CSR
Troubleshooting customer complaints	Assigning CSR to solve problem	Customer Service Supervisor (CSS)
	Establishing company liability	CSS and Legal Department
	Documenting customer's allegations	CSR
	Resolving problem, if possible, immediately	CSR
	Referring to appropriate company, department/personnel	CSR
	Tracking progress of problem solution	CSS

Exhibit 5.2.1 Skills and Incentive Matrix

Process/Step	Skills Required	CSRs have skills?		What happens?	
		Yes	No	Rewarded	Punished
Talk to customer about order or problem	Telephone skills.	✓	✓		
	Ability to interpret company policy	✓			✓
Troubleshoot customer problem	Define problem.	Not sure			✓
	Solve problem to customer's satisfaction	Not sure		✓	✓

| Procedure 5.3 | **Examine Job Designs** |

Purpose of this procedure

This procedure allows you to compare what the work group's manager and the group members think about the individual jobs in the work process. You can then identify various weaknesses in current job design.

When to use this procedure

Once skill and incentive deficits are found, you should then determine the extent that these impact individual jobs.

Before you start

1. Ask the group's manager to locate job descriptions and selection criteria for each job within the work group. (These can be informal and rough.)

2. Ask the group to review principles of work group and job design.

3. Copy Hackman and Oldham's (1980) job diagnostic survey and distribute to the group members.

4. Develop a timetable to complete this activity.

What to do

Steps	Specifics
1. Have the group's manager compare his or her job descriptions and selection criteria to the skills matrix generated in Procedure 5.2.	Ask him or her to list all differences.
2. Have each member complete a job diagnostic survey.	
3. Score the surveys and review the results with the work group's manager.	Together with the manager, list which of the following areas are weak for each job: • Skill variety — the variety of skills an employee uses • Task identity — the extent to which the job produces a "whole" identifiable output • Task significance — the job's perceived importance • Autonomy — how much discretion the job gives the employee. • Intrinsic feedback —how much the job itself indicates an employee's performance.

Exhibit 5.3 shows an example of types of weaknesses.

Exhibit 5.3 Job Weaknesses Chart: Anticipated Weaknesses, Customer Service

Areas	Job 1: Phone skills		Job 2: Troubleshoot	
	Manager Comments	**Work Group Comments**	**Manager Comments**	**Work Group Comments**
Skill variety	Great deal of variety, not only in the skills needed but in which ones are used with each customer: voice and diction, use of the language, questioning techniques, listening techniques, and use of judgment to consider how to classify customer wants/needs.	Not much variety, do and say virtually the same thing to each customer. Must concentrate to avoid boredom.	Fairly well defined, but there is variety. Must use procedure well to ensure customer satisfaction.	Have to "wing it" with most customers since guidelines don't work well with individuals. Have to think on our feet — or seat.
Task identity	Work can become sloppy, particularly at shift end. Even our best people often miss an opportunity or fail to understand what the customer wants.	Too many exceptions to the rule. What we should have is the ability to decide what to do for each customer. We really don't do as much as we could do as well as we should.	For some reason our people treat this process as if it were heuristic. They don't use the steps in the order given. As a result, the process takes too long and erodes customer satisfaction.	The procedure doesn't work. The handoffs are too clumsy and other departments are reluctant about getting involved. As a consequence we have to run from one place to another asking for favors. When it looks like we've got everything in line the supervisor takes over and finishes the job.
Task significance	Critical. Without it a person can't do the job.	Critical. We must be able to use the phone well.	Critical. Both company and customers depend on the CSR to do this well.	Very important. About the only way customers can get satisfaction.

(continued on next page)

Exhibit 5.3 *(cont.)*

Areas	Job 1: Phone skills		Job 2: Troubleshoot	
	Manager Comments	**Work Group Comments**	**Manager Comments**	**Work Group Comments**
Autonomy	Yes. When CSRs start to talk to a customer, they must operate alone. What they choose to say is up to them (given they are within company guidelines.)	Depends on CSR. Some have a supervisor listening all the time, never know when the supe (snoop) will interrupt with a comment.	At times. If the trouble is minor or easily corrected, CSR does it. Other times they call for supervisor or manager to support.	Must always bring in supervisor. Supe usually takes over.
Intrinsic feedback	Very high. Customers say what they feel is good or bad.	Most feedback from customers is negative. Usually they don't comment on our telephone skills unless they have something bad to say.	Not only what the customer says but the paperwork documenting each problem addressed.	Garbage from customers, supervisor takes the customer's side. So-called anecdotal record is a farce. We usually make them up at the end of the shift.

Prioritize Problems

Purpose of this procedure

This procedure has the entire work group come face-to-face with the problems discovered in its process and its jobs. The group is then asked to use the results from the previous procedures to prioritize which problems to solve in order to have the greatest impact on meeting its outcomes.

When to use this procedure

This is the last procedure in the analysis phase. It relies on the results of the previous work to focus the design effort on the areas of greatest value to the process's improvement.

Before you start

1. Review the group's desired outcomes (Procedure 2.1) and its goals and objectives from the environmental analysis (Procedure 3.2).

2. Make copies for the group members of the problems identified in the technical process analysis and throughout Procedures 5.1 to 5.3.

3. Compile the members' lists of the principles of process, work group, and job design that are missing or violated in the current system.

What to do

Steps	Specifics
1. Ask the group's manager to share the "ahas" found in reviewing results of the survey.	Facilitate limited discussion on these "ahas" with the group members.
2. Using previous results, identify significant problems in the process.	Ask, discuss, and record answers to the following questions: • How near to the line of action do coordination and decision making occur? • How seamless and timely are process handoffs? • How effective are existing selection, training, and reward practices? Do they —Select people with appropriate skills? —Train and develop people enough to create flexibility and the ability to troubleshoot? —Reward appropriately? • Do the values and norms of the manager and the work group reward progress?

(continued on next page)

3. Review the problem lists developed for the analysis of the technical process and for that of the human structures and systems.

4. Review the principles of process, work group, and job design that seem to be missing or violated in the current system.

5. Discuss how these problems and poor designs impact the group's desired outcomes, goals, and objectives.

   See the "Before you start" section of this procedure.

6. Rank the problems.

   Ask these questions:

   - Which problems have the greatest impact on desired outcomes, goals, and objectives?

   - Which problems matter most to customers?

   - Which problems does the work group (or manager) have the authority and resources to change?

   - Which problems can the work group (or manager) *get* the authority and resources to change?

7. Distill the entire list of problems down to a shortened list of actionable, high-impact items to resolve.

Exhibit 5.4 shows a sample of the problems that might be uncovered as a result of this procedure.

Exhibit 5.4 Problem Definition

Problem Statement	Impact	Importance to Customer	Probability We Can Change	Probability Company Can Change	Comments/ Overall Priority
Supervisors interfere with CSR autonomy.	H	H	H/L	L/H	Can change internally if jobs remain the same. H
Supervisors listen in on CSR conversations with customers without CSR's knowledge.	M	L	H	L	M
Troubleshooting procedure is impersonal and clumsy, hard to use.	M	H	M	H	Time and skills to design and develop aren't possessed internally. H
Job has very little positive intrinsic feedback.	M	L	L	L	L
Manager doesn't seem to be well informed about day-to-day operations in Customer Service.	H	M	H	H	M

H = high

M = medium

L = low

CHAPTER 6

Goal Design: Matching Work Group Goals to Environmental Demands

Since completing its initial definition of desired outcomes, the group has learned more about its customers and work environment. Group members have probably also thought more deeply about what it takes to create the product or service from both technical and human perspectives. Consequently, your role now is to help the group members incorporate this richer, deeper vision of their desired outcomes into measurable goals.

Purpose of this chapter

Just as in Procedure 2.1, "Define Desired Outcomes," the purpose of this chapter is to help the manager and work group envision what they want for the future. In this chapter, the group will answer these fundamental questions:

- What business results should we be achieving?
- What customers should we serve?
- What products and services should we offer each customer?
- From our customers' perspective, what does a quality product or service look like?
- From a work group member's perspective, what quality of work life level is needed to produce quality products or services?
- How will we measure how close we're coming to our desired outcomes?

Again, your role is to help them see their work process at its best. After they've captured this vision, they'll translate it into goals. Then you'll guide the group into making a transition from the expansive thinking they've used for their brainstorming to the practical, nitty-gritty thinking they'll need to define measures to help reach their goals. You'll ask them to find ways to keep score on the things that really matter.

How is this chapter organized?

To perform these activities:	Follow this procedure:
• Set design goals.	Procedure 6.1 — Set Goals for the Design
• Reassess the processes chosen for design.	
• Define business results.	
• Determine appropriate measures.	
• Identify desired quality of work life.	
• Decide if the design should	Procedure 6.2 — Determine the Scope of the Design
—Receive fine-tuning	
—Imitate another group's design	
—Be started from scratch	

Results

The group has set goals, established measures to track its progress, and agreed on the scope of the design. Once the group members have set their sights on where they want to go, they can design the route to get them there. In the next chapter they will design the technical route that will lead them to their destination.

For More Information

Chang, R. Y. "Continuous Process Improvement," *Info-Line* (published by the American Society of Training and Development), October 1992. Explains the tools and steps of process improvement.

Cummings, T. and Huse, E. *Organizational Development and Change,* 4th ed. (St. Paul, Minn.: West, 1989).

Galbraith, J. R. *Organization Design* (Reading, Mass.: Addison-Wesley, 1977), pp. 174–184. Describes how to select coordination mechanisms based on the information processing requirements of the task.

Goal/QPC. *The Memory Jogger: A Pocket Guide of Tools for Continuous Improvement* (Methuen, Mass, 1988). Explains the tools and steps of process improvement.

Hackman, J. R. and Oldham, G. R. *Work Redesign* (Reading Mass.: Addison-Wesley, 1980). Chapter 6, "Creating and Supporting Enriched Work," provides recommendations for designing more involving jobs (pp. 130–158).

Hammer, M. and Champy, J. *Reengineering the Corporation* (New York: Harper Business, 1993). Chapter 3, "Rethinking Business Processes" describes principles of process design (pp. 50–64). Chapter 4, "The New World of Work," describes principles of work design (pp. 65–82). Chapter 7, "The Hunt for Reengineering Opportunities," describes how to decide which processes to design (pp. 117–133). Chapter 8, "The Experience of Process Redesign," describes, in general, how to design processes (pp. 134–147).

Hanna, D. P. *Designing Organizations for High Performance* (Reading, Mass.: Addison-Wesley, 1988). Chapter 4, "The Design Process"; and Chapter 5, "Approaches to Specific Design Issues," describe the design process (pp. 92–157).

Harbour, J. L. "Improving Work Processes." *Performance and Instruction,* February 1993, pp. 5–10. Provides principles of process design and explains how to improve processes.

Lawler, E. E. *The Ultimate Advantage* (San Francisco: Jossey-Bass, 1992). Chapter 4, "Identify Work Design Alternatives"; and Chapter 5, "Develop Involving Work," explain how to design work groups and jobs (pp. 77–121). Chapter 7, "Pay the Person, Not the Job," and Chapter 8, "Reward Performance," explain compensation and reward strategies (pp. 144–201). Chapter 9, "Promote Open Information Channels," describes goals of high-involvement information systems (pp. 205–224). Chapter 10, "Establish High-Involvement Management Practices," describes high-involvement human resources systems (pp. 225–253).

Lytle, W. O. *Socio-Technical Systems Analysis and Design Guide for Linear Work* (Plainfield, N.J.: Block Petrella Weisbord, 1991). Part 6, "The New Organization Design," describes how to design a work system (pp. 99–144).

Miller, L. M. and Howard, J. *Managing Quality Through Teams* (Atlanta: Miller Consulting Group, 1991). Chapter 3, "Managing the Process," describes how to improve processes (pp. 43–66). Chapter 4, "Scorekeeping for Self-Management," describes how to select performance measures (pp. 67–84). Chapter 12, "Managing Human Performance," describes how to form a performance management system (pp. 199–222).

Mohrman, S. A. and Cummings, T. G. *Self-Designing Organizations* (Reading, Mass.: Addison-Wesley, 1989). Chapter 7, "Approaches to Designing"; and Chapter 8, "Guidelines for Designing," describe how to establish the design's scope and how to design congruent elements (pp. 87–104).

| Procedure 6.1 | **Set Goals for the Design** |

Purpose of this procedure

Using the rich data from the analysis phase, the group is ready to set its goals for the future. The goals it sets as a collective will be measurable and will directly reflect its chosen outcomes.

When to use this procedure

Having completed the procedures in the analysis phase, the group should now have a solid collection of data on which to set its goals for the new system. Additionally, the goals can be more readily developed after the specific problems have been identified in the current system.

Before you start

1. Retrieve and review:

   • The group's desired outcomes (Procedure 2.1)

   • Business environment matrix (Procedure 3.2)

   • The revised goals and objectives for the work process to be designed (Procedure 3.2)

2. Distribute the information listed above to the expanded group (the work group members, their manager, and those who will be influenced by potential structural changes). Ask them to highlight areas that they'd like to change and bring this information with them to the design goal–setting meeting.

3. Have the work group's manager list the parameters within which the design goals must fall. Parameters could include things like

   • The internal or external customers the group must serve.

   • Customer requirements of the products or services the group produces.

   • Business strategies and objectives the group must support.

   • Nonnegotiable resource limitations.

4. Prepare for a brainstorming meeting. Create an activity that gets the group to visualize what success will look like one to two years into the future.

What to do

Steps	Specifics
1. Have participants imagine they have accomplished everything they hoped for and are supporting the organization's business strategy.	Ask them to describe what they're producing and what the work process looks, sounds, and feels like.
2. Review their initial goals and the other information you distributed in the "Before you start" section.	Ask these questions: • What business results should you achieve? • What customer groups do you want to serve? • What products and/or services do you want to provide for each customer group?
3. If the group analyzed more than one process, ask them to reassess which process(es) they will design.	Select the process(es) that • Are *least* effective and efficient at producing needed business results • Have the greatest impact on external customer satisfaction • Provide the best balance of potential payoff and success
4. Have the group define desired business results for their selected processes over the next year to two.	Ask these questions: • From our customers' perspective, what does a quality product or service look like? • What customer requirements do you anticipate for the future? • What competitive advantage (or unique selling position) do you want your products and services to have compared to our competitors?

(continued on next page)

Steps	Specifics
5. Have the group determine criteria to use to evaluate how well they achieve their business results.	Ask the group which of the following provide an appropriate measure of their success: • Output • Cost • Sales • Profits • Market share • Customer satisfaction • Quality • Cycle time • Waste Ask what level of each selected measure they hope to reach.
6. Using findings from the analysis phase, have the group target quality of work life that will best support the desired business results over the next year or two.	Ask these questions: • How quickly and how often must you change your work routines to respond to your customers? • How complex is your work and the technology you use to do it? • How interdependent are the parts that you each contribute to your collective products or services? • How strong are your growth needs? How long can you do an average job within this work group without becoming bored?

Steps	Specifics
7. Have the group determine criteria to use to evaluate to what extent they reached their targeted quality of work life outcomes.	Ask which of the following areas provide an appropriate measure of the quality of their work life: • Productivity • Individual and/or team performance as appraisals • Skill growth • Absenteeism, turnover, grievances • Job satisfaction as measured on the Job Diagnostic Survey • Perceptions about how well actual patterns of behavior align with desired values (Criteria based on recommendations by Cummings and Huse [1989], Cross [1993], and Lynch [1991]) Ask what level of each selected measure they hope to reach.
8. Have the group reconcile any conflicts between the quality of work life *they* desire and the quality of work life the above factors seem to indicate is attainable.	In cases of conflicting outcomes, ask the group to reach agreement on which outcome is most supportive of their desired business results.
9. Compare the desired business results and desired quality of work life with the parameters the manager compiled before the meeting.	List any conflicts. Negotiate changes to parameters or outcomes to reconcile conflicts.
10. Set goals for the new design using the above information.	

Exhibit 6.1 shows a flowchart of this procedure.

Exhibit 6.1 Set Design Goals Flowchart

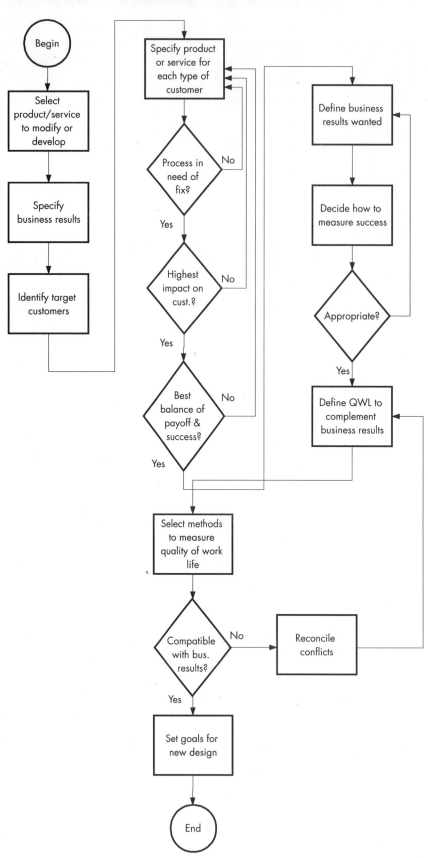

Verify the Scope of Design

Purpose of this procedure

This procedure will help you determine what level of design to pursue. The design can range from minor changes to radical change.

When to use this procedure

After you have analyzed the existing system and set your goals for design, you are ready to verify the scope of the design effort.

Before you start

1. Review the findings from the analysis phase.
2. Review the goals from Procedure 6.1.
3. If possible, refer to Mohrman and Cummings's recommendations in *Self-Designing Organizations* (1989, pp. 94–98), which these steps are based on.

What to do

Factors to Consider	Conclusions and Consequences
Determine if the existing design meets most of the group's anticipated future needs, but could be improved.	Focus on fine-tuning the current design. (The risk here is that this can lead to a "quick fix" mentality and fail to bring about significant change.)
If the existing design is not a good fit with its environment, determine if there is another work group facing similar demands that has developed an appropriate design.	Focus on imitating the exemplary group's design. (This may lessen the risks associated with innovation, but, it may not be as appropriate as it appears. It may also lead designers to focus on a program, rather than on their own process.
If there is no model design to refer to from another work group facing similar demands, proceed with a complete design starting from ground zero.	Start with a clean slate and aim for innovation rather than incremental change. (The risk is that fundamental change typically encounters significant resistance. Stakeholders who haven't been a part of the design process may reject the design.)

Exhibit 6.2 shows a decision table for choosing a design process.

Exhibit 6.2 Choosing a Design Process

If . . .	Then . . .	Risks/Problems . .
Existing design meets most of work group's anticipated future needs.	Fine-tune current design.	Can lead to a "quick-fix" mentality; might fail to bring about lasting change.
Existing design is not a good fit with its environment and another group has developed an appropriate design.	Imitate the exemplary group's design.	May lessen risk associated with innovation but may not be as appropriate as it appears. May also lead to focus on program rather than on process.
Existing design is not a good fit and there are not exemplars to imitate.	Start with a clean slate. Aim for innovation rather than incremental change.	Fundamental change typically meets with stiff resistance. Stakeholders who haven't contributed to design may reject it.

CHAPTER 7

Technical Process Design: Building Speed, Focus, and Integration into the Flow of Work

The work group is now ready to design a lean, unfragmented technical process to meet customer needs and the group's goals. You'll recall that the technical process consists of the

- Work flow

- Information flow

- Product or service specifications. (In contrast to goals for the product or service, specifications are more detailed and include interim measures throughout the process.)

A lean, unfragmented technical process is one that takes the most direct path from customer need to need-satisfying product or service. This requires streamlining, simplifying, and errorproofing the process — in general, busting bureaucracy wherever it rears its ugly head and breaking out of the rut of old habits and assumptions.

An example of a process that overcomes old assumptions is one in which customers or suppliers take over responsibility for activities they can do cheaper, better, or faster than the work group itself. For instance, in some restaurants customers make up their own salads and draw their own beverages. Hammer and Champy (1993) give the example of Wal-Mart transferring its inventory replenishment function to its suppliers. Both of these are examples of violating assumptions about organizational boundaries.

Purpose of this chapter

In designing a technical process, the work group will first identify existing rules and assumptions that place constraints on the current process. Next the group will map out a variety of different processes to meet customer requirements, *as if none of those constraints existed.* The more alternatives it considers, the more robust the ultimate design will become.

Once the team has generated multiple alternative processes, it should reconcile the new processes with the existing assumptions *only if it's impossible to eliminate or work around those assumptions.* The more imaginative the team, the better it will be at overcoming the assumptions that hamstring the current system.

In this chapter, the work group will answer these questions:

- What's the most efficient and effective way to create our products and services?

- How can we measure how well we're staying on track along the way?

How is this chapter organized?

To perform these activities:	Follow this procedure:
• Identify assumptions that might be constraining the group in producing its products or services. • Identify ways to challenge and overcome those assumptions. • Draft alternative work flows.	Procedure 7.1 — Challenge Assumptions and Map Alternative Work Flows
• Design a new work flow. • Eliminate non–value adding activities and causes of variance in the new process. • Anticipate barriers to the new process.	Procedure 7.2 — Design a New Work Flow
• Set specifications and measures for various components in the work process. • Develop a new information flow to support the process.	Procedure 7.3 — Finalize the Technical Design

Meetings

The technical design process consists of three sets of meetings with the expanded work group. The table below explains their sequence and purposes.

Meetings of:	In this sequence:	Will focus on:
Expanded work group	First set	• Listing existing assumptions and brainstorming ways to challenge them. • Mapping out a variety of work flows. • Determining the best features of each alternative.
	Second set	Reaching consensus on a single alternative work flow that integrates what the group likes best about the alternatives generated in the first set of meetings.
	Third set	Creating supporting physical work flow and information flow standards and measures.

Each set can consist of from one to several meetings, depending on

- The amount of time participants can devote to each meeting
- The complexity of the process
- The extent of experience the members have
- The extent to which they agree about how work gets done

Results

In designing the technical process, the group will identify

- The work flow needed to meet its goals most effectively and efficiently
- The information flow needed to support the work flow and facilitate decision making
- The process measures it will use to verify that its goals are being met

Once the group has designed the technical process, it can design a congruent human structure and the appropriate support systems.

For More Information

Chang, R. Y. "Continuous Process Improvement" *Info-Line* (published by the American Society of Training and Development), October 1992. Explains the tools and steps of process improvement.

Galbraith, J. R. *Organization Design* (Reading, Mass.: Addison-Wesley, 1977). Describes how to select coordination mechanisms based on the information processing requirements of the task (pp. 174–184).

Goal/QPC. *The Memory Jogger: A Pocket Guide of Tools for Continuous Improvement* (Methuen, Mass., 1988). Explains the tools and steps of process improvement.

Hanna, D. P. *Designing Organizations for High Performance* (Reading, Mass.: Addison-Wesley, 1988). Chapter 4, "The Design Process," and Chapter 5, "Approaches to Specific Design Issues," describe the design process (pp. 92–157).

Hammer, M. and Champy, J. *Reengineering the Corporation* (New York: Harper Business, 1993), Chapter 3, "Rethinking Business Processes," describes principles of process design (pp. 50–64); Chapter 4, "The New World of Work," describes principles of work design (pp. 65–82); Chapter 7, "The Hunt for Reengineering Opportunities," describes how to decide which processes to design (pp. 117–133); Chapter 8, "The Experience of Process Redesign," describes, in general, how to design processes (pp. 134–147).

Harbour, J. L. "Improving Work Processes." *Performance and Instruction,* February 1993 pp. 5–10. Provides principles of process design and explains how to improve processes.

Rummler, G. A. and Brache, A. P. *Improving Performance* (San Francisco: Jossey-Bass, 1990). Chapter 10, "Improving and Managing the Processes of the Organization," describes how to design processes (pp. 115–139).

Procedure 7.1	**Challenge Assumptions and Map Alternative Work Flows**

Purpose of this procedure

When the work group looked at its desired outcomes and started to set its goals, it began looking toward an ideal future. But during analysis group members often think of simply modifying "the way things have always been done." Now's the time to break free of "the way things have always been done."

This procedure allows the group to surface past assumptions, challenge them, and generate alternatives.

When to use this procedure

The work group will want to challenge its assumptions about the current technical process and generate alternative work flows after it has analyzed the current process, set its goals, and drafted possibilities for the future. In addition, it is often a good practice to perform this activity on a regular basis thereafter to keep the group in a state of growth.

Before you start

1. Locate the documentation from the technical process analysis:

   - Work-flow chart
   - Relationship map
   - Information-flow chart
   - Physical work-flow diagram
   - Cycle time analysis
   - Variance analysis (Section Two, Chapter 4)

2. Locate the list of group goals for the design (Section Two, Chapter 6).

2. Circle or highlight items from the above documentation that relate to the work process(es) the group will be designing.

3. Ask an information-systems professional or other process expert to join the group for its technical design meetings. Brief him or her on the above information.

4. List examples of current assumptions that limit the process. Consider assumptions about

   - What must be done to create the product or service
   - *Who* does each step
   - *When* it is done
   - *Where* it is done
   - *How* it is done
   - *Why* it is done

5. Ask the expanded group to retrieve and review the principles of process design before the meeting. Prepare a poster-size copy of the principles to post during the meeting.

6. Secure materials, including a flip chart and markers.

7. Develop a timetable to complete the procedure.

What to do

Steps	Specifics
1. Conduct a meeting with the expanded group to identify assumptions that might be constraining them in producing their products or services.	Record answers for each step below. Ask them to consider assumptions about • *What* must be done to create the product or service • *Who* does each step • *When* it is done • *Where* it is done • *How* it is done • *Why* it is done (To "prime the pump," share a few of the examples that you listed in "Before you start.")
2. Create a corresponding list with the group of ways to overcome these assumptions.	
3. Determine which ways of overcoming the assumptions would improve the work flow and be appropriate to apply to the process.	Divide flip chart pages into two columns and list assumptions in the left column and corresponding ways to overcome them in the right column. After you've finished creating the lists, ask these questions: • Which of these ways to overcome assumptions would improve the work flow or results? • Which are appropriate to apply to the work process? • Which can we do internally without help from other groups? Highlight and record the group's selections.

Steps	Specifics
4. Map alternative work flows.	Divide the group into pairs.
	Ask each pair to create and flow-chart the simplest work flow that would produce their product or service.
	Ask them to incorporate the ways of overcoming assumptions that they listed in the previous step.
	Ask the information-systems professional or process expert to circulate around the room and get the "big picture" of how the group wants the process to work. Only when a pair seems stuck should he or she make suggestions.
5. Fine-tune the flowcharts.	Ask the pairs to revise their flow-charts based on the principles of process design.
6. Determine the best features of each pair's design.	Reassemble the group and have each pair present its flowchart.
	Ask the group to discuss what it likes best about each design.
	Under each flowchart, record what the group likes best.
7. Determine the best ways to synthesize the alternatives into a single work-flow chart.	Discuss and record the group's ideas for this synthesis.
8. Develop a first-draft diagram of the synthesized flowchart.	Ask for a volunteer to work with the process expert to sketch a draft diagram of this flowchart.
	Have these two individuals reproduce each step of the flowchart on a large self-stick note and sequence the steps on a flip chart for the next meeting.

Exhibit 7.1 highlights sample assumptions identified and possible corrective actions. Exhibit 7.1.1 shows an example of a sample flowchart as an output of this procedure.

Exhibit 7.1   Work Process Assumptions: Customer Service

Assumptions	Suggested Challenge	Possible Actions from Challenge Assumptions Procedure
Supervisors are an indispensable part of the operation.	Supervisors as they operate at present may not be needed.	1. Eliminate supervisor job. 2. Train CSRs to negotiate with customers. 3. Train CSRs to troubleshoot customer complaints.
The business must have distributors for most of its products.	Using distributors adds to the cost of our products to our customers. Since we must reduce costs to remain competitive, perhaps we should deal directly with retailers.	1. Take orders from retailers directly. 2. Ship directly to retailers. 3. Change marketing strategies to support these moves. 4. Increase number of CSRs (by ten) to handle increased load. 5. Install new computer database and software to support new efforts. 6. Train CSRs to use software and deal directly with retailers.
The forms used and documentation procedures are efficient and adequate for our needs.	Transaction verification and shipping documents could be automated and shared electronically with administration and bookeeping.	1. Install new computer database and software to support new efforts. 2. Train CSRs to use software. 3. Train people in other departments to use software.

Exhibit 7.1.1   Synthesized Work-Flow Chart

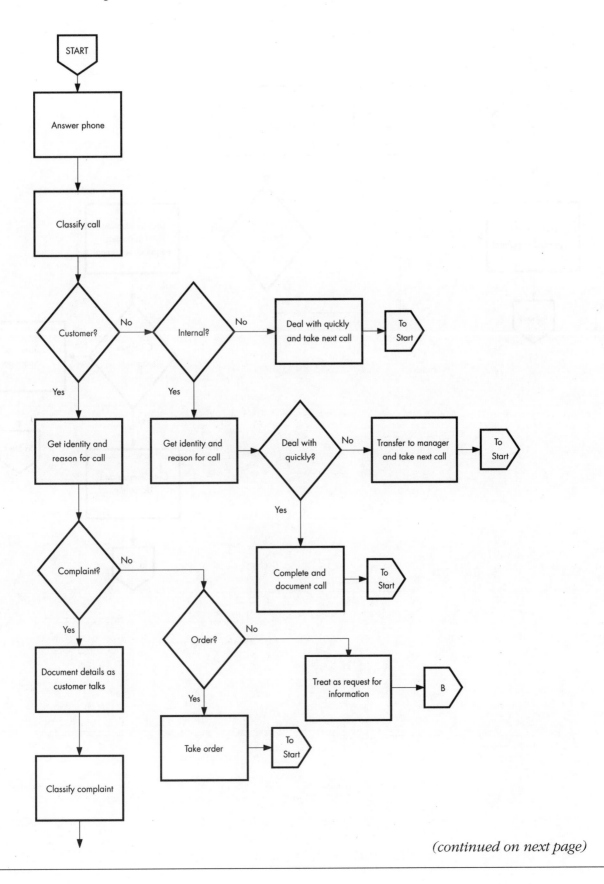

(continued on next page)

Exhibit 7.1.1 **Synthesized Work-Flow Chart** *(cont.)*

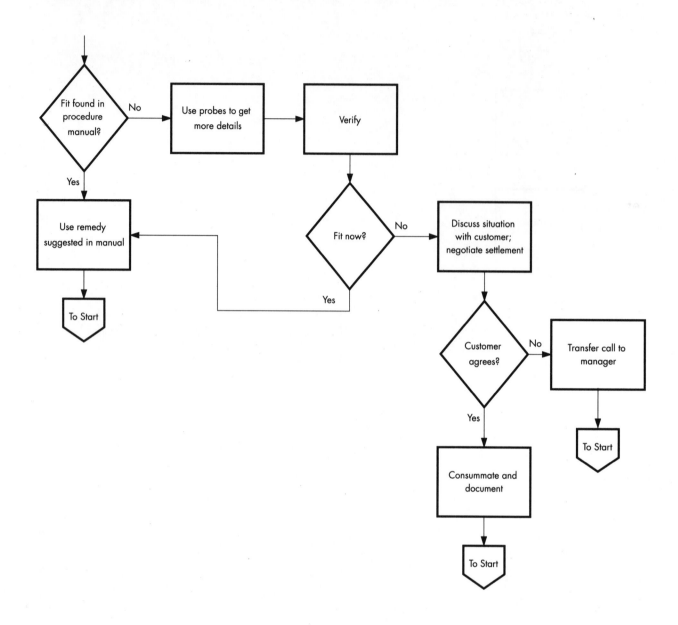

Procedure 7.2	Design a New Work Flow

Purpose of this procedure

Having selected the best features of various alternative work flows, the group is now ready to design a new and better flow. This procedure allows the group to visibly see how the work will flow and then anticipate barriers that might impede that flow.

When to use this procedure

Each group member needs to provide input into the design of a new work flow. Having had this opportunity in Procedure 7.1, the group as a whole will now be able to agree on a new design.

Before you start

1. Ask group members to bring copies of their findings from the procedures in Chapter 4 to the meeting.

2. Make sure the volunteer from the work group (from Procedure 7.1) and the information-systems professional (or process expert) are prepared for the meeting.

What to do

Steps	Specifics
Conduct a meeting with the expanded group.	Record answers for each step below.
1. Present the first-draft diagram of the new work flow.	Have the volunteer and professional or expert walk the group through the new design.
	Ask the group to identify what they like about the design.
2. Revise the design based on the principles of process design.	Ask the group to identify any changes to make based on the principles.
3. Eliminate non–value adding activities and causes of variance.	Distribute the findings about the existing process from the technical analysis.
	Ask participants to review the findings and suggest how to
	• Eliminate non–value adding activities from the cycle time analysis
	• Eliminate common causes of variances in the existing process
4. Incorporate changes to the design based on Step 3.	List, discuss, and reach a consensus on the group's suggestions.
	Distribute copies of the new work flow to the group members.

(continued on next page)

Steps	Specifics
5. Anticipate potential physical or logical barriers to the new work flow.	Ask the group for ideas about how to eliminate barriers through networking or automating work and information flow, rearranging work space, and reassigning work areas.
	(End of first meeting)
6. Before the next meeting, ask	
• that the group's manager negotiate to implement these ideas.	He or she should talk with the organization's information systems and facilities departments.
• the group members to translate their goals into end-product (or service) specifications and measures.	Refer the group to the goals it set. Make sure specifications meet their goals, anticipated customer requirements, and internal requirements and industry standards.
• group members to indicate on their new process flow-chart the locations at which interim outputs should be measured for conformance to specifications.	Measurement could occur whenever the product or service changes hands, at key decisions and interactions (for services), and at key state-changes (for products)
• group members to set the measures for these critical interim outputs.	These measures should: minimize second-party checking and controlling; indicate the absence of these variances identified in the existing process; and show that the interim output met goals, anticipated customer requirements, and industry standards.
7. Before the next meeting, ask the information-systems professional or process expert to review the new work process and compare it to the existing information flow.	

Exhibit 7.2 shows a sample of the measures for interim outputs of a customer service process.

Exhibit 7.2   Interim-Output Measures

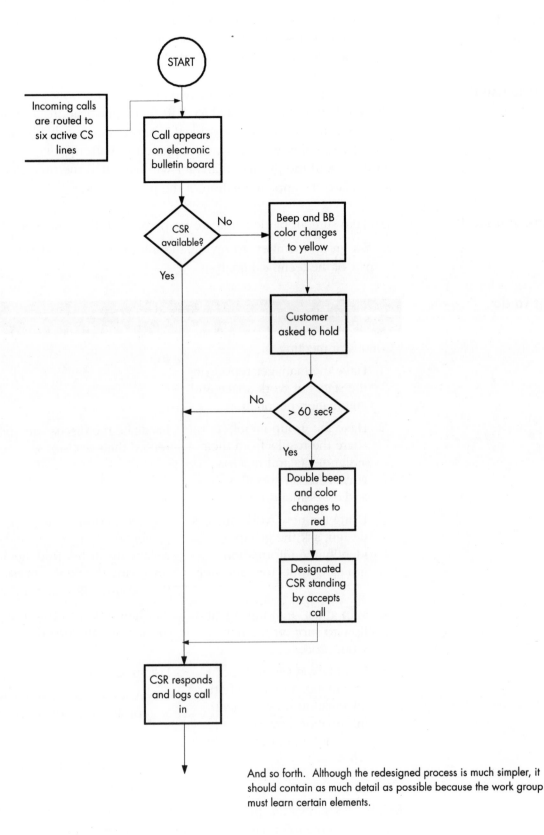

And so forth. Although the redesigned process is much simpler, it should contain as much detail as possible because the work group must learn certain elements.

| Procedure 7.3 | *Finalize the Technical Design* |

Purpose of this procedure

This procedure puts the finishing touches on the technical design. The work group will set its specifications and measures for its products and services and agree on a new information flow to support its process.

When to use this procedure

This procedure should follow the two before it. The work group members will have had the time needed to draft their specifications and measures. The information-systems professional or process expert will have had time to review the new work flow in conjunction with the existing information flow. And the group's manager will have had the time to negotiate issues related to implementation of the new process.

Before you start

1. Make sure all participants are prepared with their materials.
2. Ask group members to review the information flow, described as part of the technical analysis.

What to do

Steps	Specifics
Conduct a meeting.	
1. Have the manager report on the status of work space and automation negotiations.	
2. Have the group members share the results from their assignments and reach a consensus on specifications and assessment measures.	Facilitate the discussion and record their decisions.
3. Using the new work process design, ask the group to identify the information inputs/outputs for each step.	Ask the information-systems professional or process expert to review his or her findings from reviewing the new process and the existing information flow.
4. Map a first draft information flow to support the new work process.	Ask him or her to lead the group in mapping the first draft.
5. Identify ways to redirect, streamline, and simplify the information flow to meet information-flow principles. (See the principles in Exhibit 7.3.)	List suggestions. • Ask the information-systems professional or process expert to incorporate workable suggestions into the information-flow chart.

Exhibit 7.3 shows the principles of information flow, and Exhibit 7.3.1 shows a sample information flow through a work group.

Exhibit 7.3 Principles of Information Flow

Information flow should *provide:*

- Indicators of variances closest to the step where they occur.

- Immediate, easily accessible information and feedback so that "doers" can

  - Spot and correct variances at their point of origin

  - Make decisions or seize opportunities that their tasks present

- Information to managers so that they can coordinate efforts across processes and levels.

- A single customer contact person.

Information flow should *eliminate:*

- Ambiguous or confusing information.

- Unnecessary information.

- Unnecessary reconciliation. To cut back on the number of reconciliations, combine related documents such as receipts, invoices, and purchase orders.

Exhibit 7.3.1 Information Flow Example

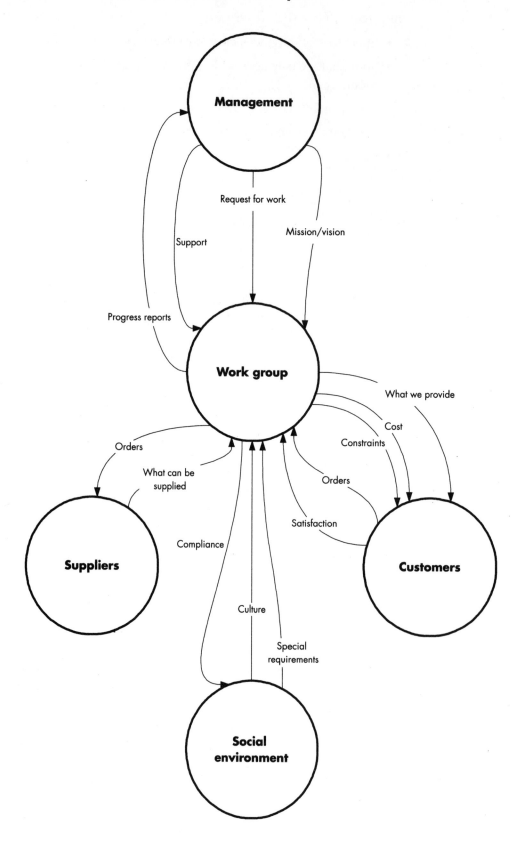

CHAPTER 8

Human Systems Design: Building Initiative and Teamwork into Jobs

You'll recall from the analysis phase that the human structures and support systems include

- Structure, lines of authority, and coordination mechanisms
- Job design
- Human resource systems
- Values and norms

Before creating the actual design, more information on these structural components should prove useful.

Structure, lines of authority, coordination mechanisms. To support a better-coordinated process, employees need the information and power to plan and control their work. Here the group must identify the information, authority, and coordination mechanisms it needs to guide and steer its work process.

Job design. To support ownership and productivity, jobs must produce whole products or services or at least discrete, coherent parts of them (*not* meaningless fragments). To produce a whole product or service within a less-fragmented work process, jobs usually need to be more comprehensive. These jobs depend on

- Employees who have a broader range of skills, including technical, managerial, administrative, and group process skills.
- Managers who have higher-level management skills. (The more the work group manages its own work process, the more a manager needs to shift from a classic supervisory role to the role of scout, strategist, and resource broker.)

Human resource systems. To support more comprehensive jobs, employees and their manager need to upgrade their skills. Ironically, one of the most common design failures is the failure to provide training in these new skills. *Before* redesigning work, organizations often assume that they can compensate for processes that don't work by providing training. This doesn't work. *After* redesigning work, organizations often assume that a good process will compensate for incompetent performers. This doesn't work either! If the new work process will require people to do things they haven't done before, they need training. Without it, the work design effort is doomed. Here the group needs guidance in identifying the skills needed for each job. A skills inventory will help determine both training needs and job selection criteria.

Values and norms. To support fast, focused, flexible performance, the work group needs feedback and reward systems that reinforce teamwork, initiative, and adaptability. To create these, the group and their manager work together with information and compensation specialists to design feedback and reward systems that guide and reinforce progress towards goals.

Purpose of this chapter

This chapter provides guidance for designing the human elements of the work process and the jobs within it. You're given a step-by-step approach to help the group, and each individual within it, determine

- How they and their work should be organized, directed, and coordinated

- How work gets distributed into individual jobs

- How people are selected, trained, evaluated, compensated, rewarded, and disciplined

- What gets rewarded (both formally and informally), as well as what people believe is important

In addition, the group will perform the following steps in the design process:

- Address values, norms, and support systems

- Plan ways to improve their jobs

- Create job profiles that incorporate these improvements

How is this chapter organized?

To perform these activities:	Follow this procedure:
• Discuss limitations of the current authority structure. • Identify changes needed for a more productive process.	Procedure 8.1 — Establish the Manager's Role in the New System
• Identify steps and specialties to add to the work flow. • Identify steps and specialties to add based on principles of work group process design. • Determine and resolve coordination problems. • Identify potential variances in the new process. • Develop a new responsibility chart.	Procedure 8.2 — Design Structure, Lines of Authority, and Coordination Mechanisms
• Identify weaknesses in current jobs. • Identify job design options. • Identify task responsibilities. • Define skill requirements and measures.	Procedure 8.3 — Design Improved Jobs
• Develop job profiles. • Determine appropriate values and norms. • Design an information/feedback system. • Design a rewards and consequences system.	Procedure 8.4 — Design Selection Criteria and Feedback, Assessment, and Rewards Systems
• Design selection practices. • Determine skill requirements. • Describe ways to develop skills.	Procedure 8.5 — Design Selection Practices and Training Systems
• Reach consensus on group composition, coordination mechanisms, allocation of authority, job responsibilities, skill requirements and measures, job profiles, information/feedback system, and performance management system	Procedure 8.6 — Finalize the Human Structures and Support Systems Design Specifications

Meetings

A predesign conference and three sets of meetings are required to design the human structures and support systems. The table below explains their sequence and purposes.

Meetings of:	In this sequence:	Will focus on:
Work group's manager	First	A Predesign conference to prepare the work group's manager to discuss human structures and distribution of authority with his or her group.
Expanded group	Second	Structure, lines of authority, and coordination mechanisms.
Expanded group	Third	Job design.
Expanded group	Fourth	Setting design specifications.

Results

With the design meetings complete, the work group will have created design specifications that spell out

- The leanest, least-fragmented work flow
- The group's composition, organized around whole products or services
- Multiskilled jobs that integrate planning, decision making, and doing
- Supporting systems, including information, feedback-and-reward, and human resources systems that enable and reinforce expanded job responsibilities and prerogatives

For More Information

Beckhard, R. and Harris, R. T. *Organizational Transitions: Managing Complex Change* (Reading, Mass.: Addison-Wesley, 1987). Chapter 10, in the Responsibility Charting section, describes the responsibility charting process you will use in this chapter (pp. 104–113).

Chang, R. Y. "Continuous Process Improvement." *Info-Line* (published by the American Society of Training and Development), October 1992. Explains the tools and steps of process improvement.

Galbraith, J. R. *Organization Design* (Reading, Mass.: Addison-Wesley, 1977), pp. 174–184. Describes how to select coordination mechanisms based on the information processing requirements of the task.

Goal/QPC. *The Memory Jogger: A Pocket Guide of Tools for Continuous Improvement* (Methuen, Mass., 1988). Explains the tools and steps of process improvement.

Hackman, J. R. and Oldham, G. R. *Work Redesign* (Reading, Mass.: Addison-Wesley, 1980). Chapter 6 provides recommendations for designing more involving jobs (pp. 130–158.)

Hanna, D. P. *Designing Organizations for High Performance* (Reading, Mass.: Addison-Wesley, 1988). Chapter 4 and Chapter 5 describe the design process (pp. 92–157).

Lawler, E. E. *The Ultimate Advantage* (San Francisco: Jossey-Bass, 1992). Chapter 4 and Chapter 5 explain how to design work groups and jobs (pp. 77–121). Chapter 7 and Chapter 8 explain compensation and reward strategies (pp. 144–201). Chapter 9 describes goals of high-involvement information systems (pp. 205–224). Chapter 10 describes high-involvement human resources systems (pp. 225–253).

Lytle, W. O. *Socio-Technical Systems Analysis and Design Guide for Linear Work* (Plainfield, N.J.: Block Petrella Weisbord, 1991). Part 6, "The New Organization Design," describes how to design a work system (pages 99–144).

Miller, L. M. *Design for Total Quality* (Atlanta: Miller Consulting Group, 1991). Chapter 5 describes how to design a work process (pp. 105–151). Chapter 6 describes how to determine work group composition and skill requirements and how to form a performance management plan (pp. 153–194).

Miller, L. M., and Howard, J. *Managing Quality Through Teams* (Atlanta: Miller Consulting Group, 19xx). Chapter 3 describes how to improve processes (pp. 43–66). Chapter 4 describes how to select performance measures (pp. 67–84). Chapter 12 describes how to form a performance management system (pp. 199–222).

| Procedure 8.1 | **Establish the Manager's Role in the New System** |

Purpose of this procedure

Before the first set of group meetings, you should prepare the work group's manager to discuss structure, lines of authority, and coordination mechanisms with the group. These will probably be sensitive issues. One of the most important reasons why new system designs fail is because managers resist them. Typically managers believe the new designs eliminate their roles. This is a good reason for resistance! The better you can explain the manager's role in the new system, the less resistance you're likely to encounter. The predesign conference will allow you to do that.

When to use this procedure

In designing the technical process, you have helped the group establish its work flow, its information flow, and its specifications and measurements. This is sufficient information to determine the scope of change and how it will affect the work group's structure, lines of authority, and coordination mechanisms. You and the manager should discuss these issues *before* the group sets out to finalize its design.

Before you start

1. Locate the documentation of your analysis of the human structures and systems. It should indicate

   - Mismatches between group boundaries and technical process boundaries

   - Recommendations of steps to add to the work group's tasks and any specialists to add to the work group

   - Mismatches between responsibility and authority

   - Coordination problems

   - Skill and incentive deficits

   - Deficiencies in job design

   (The group compiled this information in Section Two, Chapter 5.)

2. Locate the Variance Analysis Worksheet (Section Two, Chapter 4).

3. Locate the lists of group goals for business results and quality of work life. (The group created these in Section Two, Chapter 6.)

4. Circle or highlight items from the above lists that relate to the work process the group designed.

What to do

Steps	Specifics
1. Meet with the work group's manager to discuss reasons why the current authority structure won't help the group reach its goals.	Since the manager participated in the analysis, this discussion should come as no surprise.
2. Outline the kinds of changes that a more productive process requires of everyone.	The work group will take on new responsibilities. They will need their manager's guidance in planning, scheduling, budgeting, etc.
	At first the manager will have his or her hands full bringing the work group up to speed on their new process-management tasks.
	As the group becomes more skilled in doing the things that the manager used to do for them, the manager's role will shift from hands-on supervisor to scout, strategist, and resource broker.
	The more the group focuses on their own process, the more they need their manager to
	• *Scout* for "early warning signs." These could include changes in internal politics, technology, the competitive or regulatory environment, or the labor force.
	• *Strategize.* Guide and coach the group in how to handle the above changes.
	• *Broker resources* from the larger organization. Provide the information and feedback that the group needs to use these resources wisely.
3. Ask the manager for his or her concerns about changes in structure, lines of authority, and coordination mechanisms.	Help the manager put his or her concerns into words and develop coping strategies to deal with them.
4. Have the manager list parameters within which the group's human structures and systems must fall.	

Exhibit 8.1 shows what traditional management style looks like. Exhibit 8.1.1 shows an example of a modern approach to a manager's role.

Exhibit 8.1   An Old Management Style

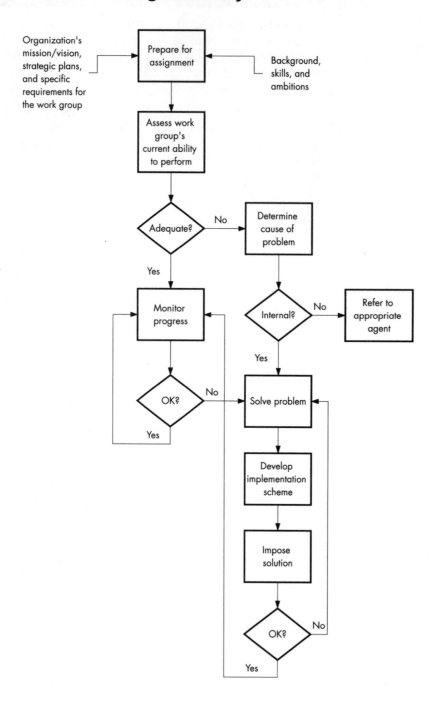

Exhibit 8.1.1   A Modern Approach to Management

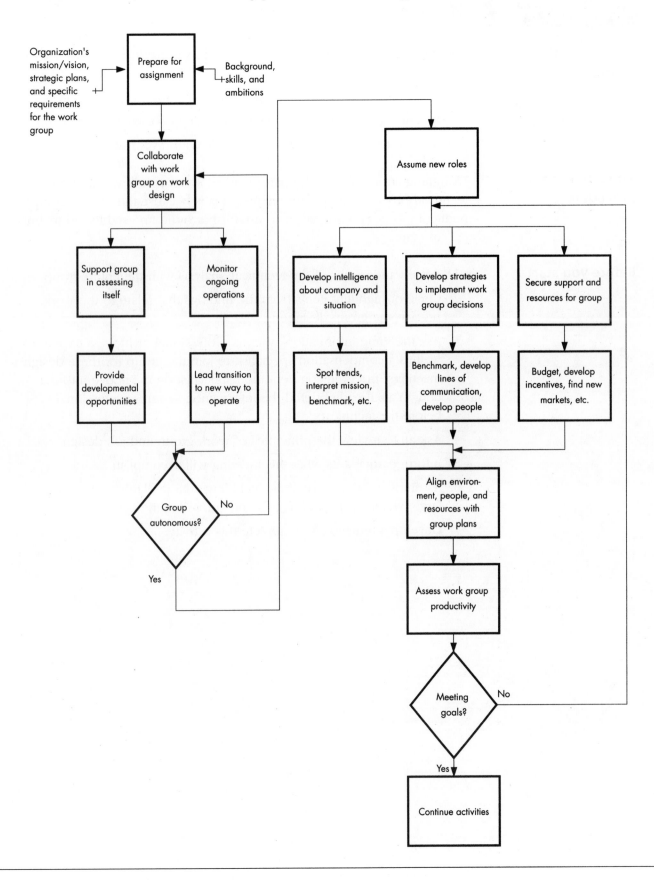

| Procedure 8.2 | # Design Structure, Authority, and Coordination Mechanisms |

Purpose of this procedure

Use the results from the analysis phase in this procedure to allow the expanded group to

- Determine a new group composition
- Identify appropriate strategies for handling coordination problems
- Identify the authority that corresponds with responsibility

When to use this procedure

Designing structures and human resource systems follows design of the technical processes and components. This is because the human components of job design are easier to establish around an established technical structure.

Before you start

1. Review the results of the technical analysis with the entire group.
2. Circle or highlight items from the findings that relate to the work process the group designed.
3. Ask the same information-systems professional or process expert, as well as a compensation specialist, to join the group for these design meetings. Brief the compensation specialist on the above information. (You already briefed the information-systems professional before the technical design.)
4. Ask all to review the principles of work group and job design.
5. Inform participants what this meeting will accomplish.
6. Assemble working materials, including a large blank surface (e.g., a large whiteboard or flip chart) and colored markers.
7. Develop a timetable to complete this activity.

What to do		
	Steps	**Specifics**

1. Ask the group to retrieve and review the lists they've compiled of

   - Mismatches between group boundaries and technical process boundaries

   - Recommended steps to add to the work group's tasks

   - Recommended specialties to add to the work group

   - Coordination problems

2. Identify steps and specialties to integrate into the new workflow design based on the principles of work group design.

   Post the principles of work group design.

   Ask the group what steps and specialties need to be integrated based on these principles.

   Record their answers.

3. Identify ways to integrate the needed new steps and specialties into the new work flow design.

   Use the results from Procedure 5.2 to guide the discussion.

   Record their answers.

4. Determine coordination problems.

   Ask the group to retrieve and review coordination problems with their existing process.

   Ask them to mark those coordination problems they think would *still* occur in the new work process. (The above integration mechanisms should eliminate most coordination problems.)

   Ask them to list any new coordination problems that are likely to occur in the new process.

   In the left column of a two-column flip chart page, list the coordination problems.

(continued on next page)

Steps	Specifics
5. Identify appropriate coordination mechanisms to establish.	Post the following list of coordination mechanisms: • Rules and methods • Hierarchy • Plans • Direct contact between managers of areas involved in coordination • Liaison roles • Boundary-spanning teams • Dedicated integrator roles • Matrix organization (List based on coordination alternatives described by Galbraith [1977], pp. 175–176.) Ask the group to identify appropriate coordination mechanisms for their coordination problems. Tell them the more complex and unpredictable the coordination problem, the farther down on the coordination mechanisms list they should go. List their choices on the right column of the flipchart
6. Identify any new variances that might occur in the new process.	Ask the group to retrieve and review the variance analysis worksheet. Ask them to mark any existing variances that might still occur in the new process. Ask them to list any new variances that they anticipate.

Steps	Specifics
7. Develop a new responsibility chart.	Sketch a responsibility chart on a flip chart.
	List the steps of the new work process in the left column.
	Ask the group to fill in the cells so that they
	• Provide the person who controls each anticipated variance with the authority and responsibility to fix it.
	• Provide each member with authority appropriate to their responsibilities.
	• Define roles sufficiently to avoid overlapping responsibilities. (If more than one member has responsibility for a task, specify when each member should act.)
8. Facilitate the group in reaching consensus about allocation of responsibility.	Ask the group's manager to discuss the group's responsibility chart and compare it to his or her list of parameters. (He or she developed these at the predesign conference.)
	Ask whether any group members' responsibilities need to change to fit those parameters.

Exhibit 8.2 shows one type of worksheet to use to determine responsibilities.

Exhibit 8.2   Responsibility Development Worksheet: Task/Skill Matrix

New Job: Customer Advocate

Defined: A customer advocate is a person within the company (Customer Service) who takes the part of the customer during disputes over complaints, service, etc. S/he is charged with the responsibility of interpreting company policy and procedures for the customer to understand. S/he must then develop (through negotiation) a compromise position acceptable to both the customer and the company. The goal is a win/win solution.

Task	*Skills*	*Resources*	*Outcomes*
Clarify and/or define the problem.	Probe, paraphrase, explain.	Time in process.	All vested parties have common understanding of the problem and the customer's attitudes and values that are in conflict.
Present customer's point of view and motivation to company representative.	Basic communication skills.	Materials such as flip charts and overhead transparencies as needed.	Company representative can understand customer's point of view and motivation.
Provide venue for confrontation or discussion.	Skills to arrange sessions and facilitate meetings.	Conference room C. Third-party phone call. Teleconferencing equipment.	Both parties feel they are being treated well and fairly.
Act as mediator.	Basic negotiation skills. Note taking. Documentation	Time in process.	Discussion is even; neither party has advantage. Each is afforded ample opportunity to explain or debate each point.
Act as advocate.	Basic communication skills.	Time in process.	The customer finds himself/herself with an ally.
Negotiate settlement on behalf of customer.	Basic negotiation skills.	Depends on nature and outcome of the session. Replace goods, refund money (other appropriate to the settlement), or nothing.	Customer leaves session fully satisfied that s/he has received full courtesy and fair treatment. Feels it was a win/win deal.

Note: The process has two phases. In the initial phase the customer advocate acts as a neutral to insure that the interaction does not become acrimonious or that no important information is lost. In the second phase, the customer advocate takes the position of the customer and negotiates on his/her behalf.

| Procedure 8.3 | **Design Improved Jobs** |

Purpose of this procedure

This procedure allows you to design jobs based on the needs of the individuals in the work group, their managers, and the group as a whole. The group will

- Identify weaknesses in current jobs
- Identify job design options
- Identify task responsibilities
- Define skill requirements and measures

When to use this procedure

Structure, lines of authority, and coordination mechanisms should be in place before looking at the individual jobs in the new process. They set the parameters for each of the jobs the group will now design.

Before you start

1. Before you meet with the group as a whole for the second set of human design meetings, ask the manager to retrieve and review the job diagnostic survey (JDS) findings.

2. Meet one-on-one with the manager to discuss weaknesses in current jobs and job design options. Explain the options listed on page 164.

3. Assemble materials, including a flip chart and markers.

4. Develop a timetable to complete this activity.

To provide:	Do this:
Identity or "wholeness"	Define jobs around whole products or services, or at least discrete, coherent parts.
Skill variety	• Crosstrain employees and rotate jobs. • Add technical steps to the job, such as troubleshooting. • Add process-management tasks to the job, such as planning, scheduling, and budgeting. • Establish direct relationships between workers and customers.
Meaning/importance	• Define jobs around whole, value-adding outputs and natural or logical groupings of tasks. • Provide each jobholder with the "big picture," explaining how his or her part contributes to customer satisfaction. • Establish direct relationships between workers and customers.
Autonomy	• Establish direct relationships between workers and customers. • Vertically load job (push down responsibility and authority, integrate planning and controlling with doing).

Intrinsic feedback	• Establish direct relationships between workers and customers.
	• Make sure feedback goes directly to the person who's responsible for the step, product, or service. Remove barriers or blocks that isolate employees from knowledge of results.
	   —Make workers responsible for quality control.
	   —Provide performance reports directly to workers.
	   —Automate feedback.

(Based on Hackman and Oldham's recommendations [1980, pp. 130–158].)

What to do

Steps	Specifics
1. Identify weaknesses of current jobs.	Review results of the JDS.
	Post the responsibility chart the group developed in the previous meeting.
	Ask the group to identify weaknesses in their current jobs that they believe would *still* exist within the new allocation of responsibility.
	In the left column of a two-column flip chart page, list the job weaknesses.
2. Identify job design options.	Post the same list of design options that you explained to the manager before the meeting.
	Ask the group to identify appropriate design options for each job weakness.
	List their choices in the right column.
3. Facilitate the group and manager in reaching consensus on appropriate job design options.	Post the principles of job design.
4. Identify task responsibilities.	Ask each group member to come up with a list of tasks or steps for which he or she is individually responsible, based on the • Responsibilities identified in the responsibility chart • Design options the group agreed upon • Principles of job design
5. Facilitate the group in reaching consensus on their job lists.	Have individuals share their lists with the group.

(continued on next page)

Steps	Specifics

6. Define skill requirements and measures for newly defined jobs.	Have individuals work alone.
	
	Point out that more comprehensive jobs require skills in
	
	• Tracking and assessing the business environment and adjusting performance appropriately
	
	• Troubleshooting the work process
	
	• Managing the work process, including planning, scheduling, budgeting, and staffing
	
	• Leading and contributing to a work group. Group process skills include:
	   —Facilitating meetings
	   —Problem solving
	   —Negotiating
	   —Decision making
	   —Resolving conflict

7. Facilitate the group in reaching consensus on skill requirements and measures.	Have individuals share their skill requirements and measures with the group.
8. Schedule meetings to develop corresponding support systems. Break the group into two smaller groups as shown on right. Explain that group 2 will use the results from group 1 to perform its task.	(see table below)

Assign this group:	To draft these support systems:	Include these players:
Group 1	Selection criteria and feedback, assessment, and reward systems.	• Group manager • Compensation specialist • Information systems professional • Experienced work group members
Group 2	Selection practices and training systems	• You (or another training specialist) • Experienced work group members

Exhibit 8.3 shows an example of new job requirements.

Exhibit 8.3   Task/Skill Matrix

New Job: Customer Advocate

Defined: A customer advocate is a person within the company (Customer Service) who takes the part of the customer during disputes over complaints, service, etc. S/he is charged with the responsibility of interpreting company policy and procedures for the customer to understand. S/he must then develop (through negotiation) a compromise position acceptable to both the customer and the company. The goal is a win/win solution.

Task	Skills	Resources	Outcomes
Clarify and/or define the problem.	Probe, paraphrase, explain.	Time in process.	All vested parties have common understanding of the problem and the customer attitudes and values that are in conflict.
Present customer's point of view and motivation to company representative.	Basic communication skills.	Materials such as flip charts and overhead transparencies as needed.	Company representative can understand customer's point of view and motivation.
Provide venue for confrontation or discussion.	Skills to arrange sessions and facilitate meetings.	Conference room C. Third-party phone call. Teleconferencing equipment.	Both parties feel they are being treated well and fairly.
Act as mediator.	Basic negotiation skills. Note taking. Documentation.	Time in process.	Discussion is even; neither party has advantage. Each is afforded ample opportunity to debate each point.
Act as advocate.	Basic communication skills.	Time in process.	The customer finds himself/herself with an ally.
Negotiate settlement on behalf of customer.	Basic negotiation skills.	Depends on nature and outcome of the session. Replace goods, refund money (other appropriate to the settlement), or nothing.	Customer leaves session fully satisfied that s/he has received full courtesy and fair treatment. Feels it was a win/win deal.

Note: The process has two phases. In the initial phase the customer advocate acts as a neutral to insure that the interaction does not become acrimonious or that no important information is lost. In the second phase, the customer advocate takes the position of the customer and negotiates on his/her behalf.

Design Selection Criteria and Feedback, Assessment, and Rewards Systems

Purpose of this procedure

This procedure asks the members in subgroup 1 (from Procedure 8.3) to develop a job profile for each job, including the social and growth needs that job candidates should have. They will also determine appropriate values and norms. Finally, the group will design the appropriate information/feedback and assessment/reward systems for the work group.

When to use this procedure

Once the new jobs are designed, the group can more easily identify the necessary support systems it will need.

Before you start

1. Tell the group that their purpose is to develop a job profile for each job. In addition to the skill requirements and assessment criteria that the group has already developed for each job, they should profile the social and growth needs that the ideal candidate for this job should have. Explain that

   • To succeed in jobs requiring multiple skills, contributors need to find skill growth motivating. Employees who do *not* value skill growth will *not* fit well in comprehensive jobs.

   • To succeed in jobs where a team, *not* an individual, performs the work process, contributors need to find interpersonal interaction motivating. If employees like to work as "lone rangers" and do *not* value taking part in a collective effort, they will *not* fit well in team-based jobs.

2. Provide a time limit to the meeting.

What to do

Steps	Specifics
1. Develop job profiles.	Explain they must take into account the social and growth needs for the jobs.
2. Profile appropriate values and norms for newly defined jobs.	
3. Draft the specifications for an information/feedback system.	Ask the information-systems specialist to lead the group in creating specifications for the system to support the new design.

Remind the group to incorporate

- Information flow (Section Two, Chapter 4)

- Business results and goals for quality of work life goals (Section Two, Chapter 6)

- Product or service specifications for final and interim outputs (Section Two, Chapter 2)

- Job skill requirements and measures (Procedure 8.3)

(continued on next page)

Steps	Specifics
4. Finalize the specifications.	As the information-systems professional completes the specifications, have him or her walk the group through them.

Ask the group to provide feedback on

- The overall business context, including
  - —Market demand
  - —Business cycles
  - —Forces that influence business performance
  - —Business performance
- The technical process including measures of
  - —How well outputs are meeting customer requirements and industry or professional standards
  - —What variances occur, and when, where, and why they occur.
  - —How well individual skills support the tasks that contribute to the work process.
- The human structure and systems including measures to give feedback on:
  - —How well the system is meeting criteria for quality-of-work life outcomes.
  - —How well the group's actions support the values established for newly defined jobs.

Steps	Specifics

5. Draft reward and compensation systems.

   Ask the group to brainstrom ways to recognize and reward accomplishment for their most important measures.

To "prime the pump" you can suggest any of the following that the compensation specialist says are workable within the group's division.

To reward or compensate for:	Consider:
Organizational performance	Profit sharing–type compensation
Work group results	Pay for performance (if the team performs the work process, use *team*-based pay)
Broad-based skill development	Pay for skill (*individual*-based pay)
Teamwork and support of vision and values	Special recognition, assignment to roles involving leadership and group facilitation

6. Identify the consequences of failing to reach targeted measures and identify a performance-management system to address such failure.

   Ask the group to brainstorm consequences of low or poor performance.

7. Ask the compensation specialist to indicate which items on the brainstormed list are workable in the group's division.

8. Finalize rewards and consequences.

   Have the group select from its lists those rewards and consequences that

   - Reward results, *not* activity. (Include interim outputs as results.)

   - Pay for performance and promote for ability.

   - Reward for satisfying customers, *not* for protecting turf or building empires.

Exhibit 8.4 shows a sample of what new job attributes might look like.

Exhibit 8.4   New Job Attributes

New Job: Customer Advocate, p.2

Business Context			
Market Demand	**Business Cycle**	**What influences performance?**	**Business Performance**
Customers find it increasingly difficult to get a fair hearing or even to make themselves heard. Our customer advocates will provide a means for them to better understand us and what we can do for them.	Job has its largest contribution at the beginning of cycle and after the sale. At beginning CAs can provide marketing and management with valuable information and insights about current customer preferences and demands. Should save about 30% of need for market analysis. Main thrust at end where the nitty-gritty work will be done.	CA gets positive feedback from customers and executive management. Production, shipping, and distribution will usually react poorly (since they're most likely to be criticized). Colleagues in Customer Service who represent the company during negotiations are important teammates and will probably appreciate the contributions of the CA because they won't have to "coddle" customers. Whole customer service team will benefit.	The benefits to the business are • Increased customer loyalty. • Good public relations. • Dollar increases due to better trust/dependence. • Large (at least 20%) decrease in liability costs due to litigation. Drawbacks include • Increased cost for replacement and refurbishment of merchandise. Expect 10%. • Increased salary costs for CAs.

Human Structure		Rewards	
Quality of Work Life	**Work Group Support**	**Salary**	**Other**
This job may be stressful since the CA is a key member of the Customer Service team who must settle customer complaints about Customer Service. It will also require a great deal of preparation and getting to know the customer. There should be meaningful relations outside the company.	The Customer Service people have to support the CAs or the job won't be performed well. Suggest management provide intensive training in what the job is and how valuable it can be to the company.	Salary should be that of a senior CSR plus an increment of 12% to account for the added skills and responsibilities.	Professional dues paid to local chapter of a recognized association for negotiators or arbitrators. Expenses to one national conference per year.

Procedure 8.5 — Design Selection Practices and Training Systems

Purpose of this procedure

This procedure establishes the selection practices that give work group members a stake in a new employee's success. In addition, the group will compare their existing skills with those necessary for the newly designed jobs. The gap between these will identify the training or performance support needed by the group or its individual members.

When to use this procedure

Once job profiles have been developed, appropriate values and norms identified, and appropriate information/feedback and assessment/reward systems designed, you are ready to specify the selection practices and performance support systems most suitable to the group.

Before you start

1. Have subgroup 2 review the job profiles that subgroup 1 developed.

2. Provide a time limit for the meeting.

What to do

Steps	Specifics
1. Draft selection practices. Ask the group to brainstorm selection practices that give work group members a stake in a new member's success.	To get them started, you can offer these suggestions: • Provide candidates with a *realistic* job preview or walk through. • Have work group members interview and select new members. • Have work group members orient new members to the work as well as group values and norms.
2. Facilitate the group in reaching consensus on which of the above practices they wish to adopt.	
3. Review skill requirements.	Ask the group to make sure required skills include • Tracking key business indicators and adjusting operations accordingly • Technical and maintenance skills that the work process requires • Management and administrative skills • Group process skills
4. Estimate current jobholders' existing skill levels in each of the above areas.	
5. Define the gap between the skills employees will need and the skills they currently have.	List requirements that will need training or performance support.
6. Provide recommendations on the most efficient and effective way to close the gap	Recommend appropriate training, job aids, and/or other performance supports.

Exhibit 8.5 shows a sample of gaps that might exist and recommended methods to close them.

Exhibit 8.5   Skills Gaps Identification

Application Criteria for Customer Advocates

1. Must have five years' experience as CSR or equivalent. (Equivalency could come from training or similar experience at a different company. It will be judged by the selection committee in Customer Service.)

2. Recommendations from CS manager and/or at least two colleagues not on the selection committee.

3. Candidates must have

   - Good communication (especially conversational) skills
   - Training in negotiations (may be provided by the company after selection)
   - Thorough understanding of the goods and services offered by the company and how those benefit customers

4. Candidates should

   - Have the capacity to accept criticism from colleagues without undue emotional stress
   - Be able to document and report on meetings with accuracy and fairness
   - Be able to investigate customers to establish viability and cause of claims made against the company

Summary for Lucy Martinez:

Skill Area	Extent in Hand	Gap	How to Remedy
Negotiations	Low	Large	Go to seminar, practice with friendly customer, one who knows her well and trusts her. Critical area.
Communication skills	High	Small to none	N/A
Planning skills	Low	Large, not critical	Study with Marty. Read book.
Investigation	Medium	Don't know?	Wait to see how well she is able to do the job without more effort in this area.

Procedure 8.6	*Finalize the Human Structures and Support Systems Design Specifications*

Purpose of this procedure

This procedure has the entire group put its stamp of approval on the final design specifications. Each group member has the opportunity to suggest revisions before the design is accepted.

When to use this procedure

This procedure comes last in the design of the human structure and support systems.

Before you start

1. Collect and distribute

   • The group structure, lines of authority, and coordination mechanisms developed in the first design meeting.

   • The job tasks/steps, skill requirements, and measures from the second design meeting

   • The job profiles, information-systems specifications, and recommendations for rewards and consequences from the first subgroup meeting.

   • The selection practices and training specifications from the second subgroup meeting.

2. Ask members to review this information and annotate it with their questions or suggestions for changes *before* the last set of design meetings.

3. Schedule the meeting.

What to do

Steps	Specifics

1. Revise and reach consensus on
    • Group composition
    • Coordination mechanisms
    • Allocation of authority
	Facilitate the discussion and record the results.

2. Revise and reach consensus on
    • Steps or tasks each job is responsible for
    • Job enhancements
    • Skill requirements and measures.
	Facilitate the discussion and record the results.

3. Revise and reach consensus on
    • Job profiles, including required skills, social needs, and values and norms
    • Information/feedback system specifications
    • Performance management system specifications (rewards and consequences)
    • Training specifications
	Facilitate the discussion and record the results.

4. Combine these results with the final results from Chapters 6 and 7.	These are your *design specifications!*

Note: We have not included a sample of design specifications because that would limit your thinking. Your design specifications should fit your needs based on your work group's and organization's individuality.

CHAPTER 9

Implementation: Managing the Transition from Plans to Reality

Authors typically describe implementation and evaluation as the last steps in a linear process that begins with analysis. However, implementation and evaluation *actually* begin at the same time as analysis. That's because at the same time the group determines performance criteria for the new system, they establish evaluation criteria. And as they determine what changes need to be made, they involve those who might be affected by the changes. The implementation's success depends on how thoroughly you involve those who must make the new system work. If you wait until the work group completes the design to involve affected individuals who aren't part of the work group, you will have waited *too long!*

Purpose of this chapter

This chapter explains how to form transition plans and implement changes. If you think of your design specifications as a targeted destination, you can think of the implementation process as the journey to get there. Without a carefully planned and managed transition, work group members

- Lose the time, effort, and hopes they invested in the design process
- Lose faith in their ability to achieve their aspirations and meet the challenges they face
- End up with an inadequate system with insufficient adaptive capability and more internal support

With a carefully planned and managed implementation, work group members develop

- A unified identity and a feeling of self-sufficiency
- The capacity to adapt to the challenges facing them and to achieve their goals
- Ownership over their work process and its results

Therefore, this chapter focuses on implementation. Because the work group has designed its measures and specifications, it knows what to evaluate to determine the new system's level of effectiveness. The group needs only to identify at what time to conduct its evaluations.

How is this chapter organized?

To perform these activities:	Follow this procedure:
• Strategize ways to minimize restraining forces. • List action steps for each major change. • Compile steps into action plans.	Procedure 9.1 — Draft Action Plans
• Develop a time line and resource list, and assign a project manager to each action plan.	Procedure 9.2 — Finalize Action Plans
• Try out, assess, and adapt the new system.	Procedure 9.3 — Implement and Consolidate the New System

Meetings

Two sets of meetings are needed to design the implementation plan. After the first set, group members break into subgroups. You assign change categories and further action planning to each subgroup.

Meetings of:	In this sequence:	Will focus on:
Expanded work group	First	• Estimating driving and restraining forces. • Strategizing ways to minimize restraining forces. • Categorizing major changes. • Listing action steps for each major category.
Expanded work group	Second	• Developing an overall sequence for all action plans. • Developing time lines and resource lists for each plan. • Choosing a project manager for each action plan.

Results

At this point the group has still not finished designing the process. In fact, the system is *never* finished! Work groups must continuously adapt to demands and fight back creeping complexity and unnecessary bureaucracy. Even though they cannot take comfort in having created a finished system, they can take pride in having established a *self-renewing* process, their best insurance against obsolescence.

For More Information

Beckhard, R. and Harris, R. T. *Organizational Transitions: Managing Complex Change* (Reading, Mass.: Addison-Wesley, 1987). Chapter 10, "Commitment Planning and Strategies," describes how to identify what level of commitment the change requires and presents intervention strategies to build needed commitment (pp. 91–113).

Beer, M., Eisenstat, R. A., and Spector, B. *The Critical Path to Corporate Renewal* (Boston: Harvard Business School Press, 1990). Chapter 4, "The Critical Path to Renewal," explains how to sequence different types of changes so that each change lays the necessary foundation for the next and allows adaptability appropriate to its stage in the overall change process (pp. 67–109).

Bridges, W. *Managing Transitions* (Reading, Mass.: Addison-Wesley, 1991). Describes the phases that people go through when making a major change and suggests strategies to support them in each phase.

Connor, D. *How to Be an Effective Sponsor of Major Organizational Change* (distributed by ODR). Describes key stakeholders in the change process.

Craig, D. P. *The Hip Pocket Guide to Planning and Evaluation* (San Diego: Learning Concepts, 1978). Step 4, "Preparing for Implementation," and Step 5, "Designing the Evaluation," describe how to create implementation and evaluation plans (pp. 60–107).

Hackman, J. R. and Oldham, G. R. *Work Redesign* (Reading, Mass.: Addison-Wesley, 1980). Chapter 9, "Installing Changes in Work Systems," identifies the decisions work groups must make when they decide to design work (pp. 221–244).

Hanna, D. P. *Designing Organizations for High Performance* (Reading, Mass.: Addison-Wesley, 1988). Chapter 6, "Managing Cultural Change," describes values and requirements essential to the change process (pp. 158–180).

Hammer, M. and Champy, J. *Reengineering the Corporation* (New York: Harper Business, 1993). Chapter 9, "Embarking on Reengineering," explains two elements of a design proposal, the case for action, and the vision for the future (pp. 148–158).

Kepner, C. H. and Tregoe, B. B. *The New Rational Manager.* (Princeton, N.J.: Kepner-Tregoe, 1991). Chapter 6, "Potential Problem Analysis," explains how to anticipate implementation problems and select strategies to prevent or minimize those potential problems (pp. 139–161).

Lytle, W. O. *Starting an Organization Design Effort* (Plainfield, N.J.: Block Petrella Weisbord, 1993). Chapter 6, "Readiness: Assessing the Organization's Readiness for Change," explains how to assess readiness for change and how to diagnose where an individual is in his or her progression through the phases of organizational change (pp. 105–113). Chapter 7, "Power: Building a Coalition," explains how to identify key stakeholders' current and desired level of support and how to generate strategies to move them from current to desired levels of support (pp. 123–132). Chapter 8, "Sanction: Gaining Approval," describes how to generate a change proposal (pp. 133–137). Chapter 9, "Mobilization: Preparing the Organization for Change," describes how to orient and involve stakeholders who aren't on the design team in the change process (pp. 139–146). Chapter 10, "Leadership: Getting Out in Front," describes how to establish the need for change, create energy for change, and build in the capacity for ongoing renewal (pp. 147–158).

Lytle, W. O. *Socio-Technical Systems Analysis and Design Guide for Linear Work* (Plainfield, N.J.: Block Petrella Weisbord, 1991). Part 7, "Implementation Plan," identifies components of an implementation plan (pp. 145–150).

Miller, L. M. *Design for Total Quality* (Atlanta: Miller Consulting Group, 1991). Chapter 7, "Planning Implementation," describes how to plan implementation (pp. 195–214).

Mohrman, S. A. and Cummings, T. G. *Self-Designing Organizations* (Reading, Mass.: Addison-Wesley, 1989). Chapter 12, "Guidelines for Implementing the Design," describes principles of effective change management (pp. 133–144). Chapter 13, "Guidelines for Assessing the Design," describes how to make evaluation "minimally threatening and maximally useful" (pp. 145–154).

National Society for Performance and Instruction. *Introduction to Performance Technology* (Washington, D.C., 1989). Chapter 17, "The ABCDs of Managing Change," (by Diane Dormant), describes the key stakeholders in the change process, stages that they go through in adopting an innovation, and change agent strategies appropriate to each stage of adoption (pp. 238–256).

Westgaard, O. and Hale, J. *The Competent Manager's Handbook for Measuring Unit Productivity* (Chicago: Hale Associates, 1985). Describes various methods to use when implementing and evaluating a work group's performance.

Woodward, H. and Buchholz, S. *After-shock: Helping People Through Corporate Change* (New York: Wiley, 1987). Describes the phases that organizations and individuals go through when making a major change and suggests strategies to support them in each phase.

Draft Action Plans

Purpose of this procedure

The purpose of this procedure is to plan the transition from the current system to the new system. You must plan the transition as thoughtfully as you designed the new system. It's like planning a move. You must decide what to keep, what to let go of, and how to make the move.

In *Managing Transitions,* William Bridges (1991) warns that the most common reason organizational changes fail is that those who initiate the change fail to think through and manage necessary endings and transitions. Instead they focus solely on planning the new beginning.

During the design stage the work group planned the new beginning. Now together you will plan the ending of the old and the transition to the new. You will sequence this transition so the work group can informally try out and adapt the new system before they formalize it. This allows them to try out the system in a low-risk context.

The products of this planning are draft action plans that map out the route to the new work environment.

When to use this procedure

With the analysis and design phases complete, the work group is ready to begin planning how it will implement the design. It's like any good game plan. First the team studies and practices hard. Then it enters the game ready to succeed.

Before you start

1. Locate and distribute the final design specifications. Ask the group to list the changes that will need to occur in

   - The group's goals and objectives

   - The work process, including the requirements/specifications, work flow, and information flow

   - The human organization and support systems, including structure, lines of authority, coordination mechanisms, and job design and human resources systems

   (You specified these changes when you completed the procedures in Chapters 6, 7, and 8.)

2. List those outside the work group who will influence the adoption of the new system, including those who

   - Must *approve* the system

   - Must *change* the way they work as a result of the new system

   - Must *implement* the new system

   - Can *influence* others to accept (or reject) the new system

3. Estimate what each stakeholder has to lose and gain from the change.

What to do

Steps	Specifics
Conduct the first implementation planning meeting. Follow the steps below.	
1. Identify driving and restraining forces that will influence the work group's progress towards the new system.	Create a two-column flip chart page.
	Have the group brainstorm driving and restraining forces. List driving forces in the left column and restraining forces in the right.
2. Cluster the forces into categories of similar types of influence.	Facilitate the group in categorizing the forces.
3. Ask the group to prioritize the categories by level of impact by voting.	
4. Facilitate the group in brainstorming strategies to minimize restraining forces in high-impact categories.	
5. Categorize the changes the group identified as a result of what you asked them to do in the *Before you start* section.	Ask the group to share their lists of changes that need to occur.
	List these on a flip chart, categorizing them and weeding out duplications.
6. Identify the actions needed to make the assigned changes.	Break the group into subgroups and divide the changes among the subgroups.
	Ask the subgroups to identify needed steps.
	Ask them to compile steps into a draft action plan and post their plan.
7. Improve action plans.	Have all group members circulate around the room and note on the posted pages any ideas they have to improve the other subgroups' action plans.

Steps	Specifics
8. Lead a discussion on plan strengths, ideas for improvement, and commonalities and differences.	Reassemble the members into a large group.
9. Post and review the sequencing guidelines in Exhibit 9.1.	
10. Assign subgroups to create a flowchart and relationship map for each of their action plans, based on the sequencing guidelines.	Dismiss the meeting.

Exhibit 9.1   Sequencing Guidelines

Sequence changes so the work group may *informally* try out changes in the work process and its associated roles and relationships, *before* instituting formal changes. This means the work group receives

- Objectives, preliminary role definitions, and informal reorientation of relationships *before* training.

- Training and team building *before* formal changes in appraisal systems or permanent reassignments of work team members.

- Formal changes in appraisal systems and permanent reassignments of work team members *before* formal changes in compensation and reward systems and organizational structures.

- Formal changes in compensation and reward systems and organizational structures *after* informally piloting and fine-tuning the new work process, as well as its supporting roles, relationships, and systems.

(Based on research by Beer, Eisenstat, and Spector [1990].)

Finalize Action Plans

Purpose of this procedure

This procedure takes the results of the previous procedure and finalizes the group's action plan for implementing the design. In addition, project managers are assigned to oversee each plan.

When to use this procedure

Once action plans have been drafted and new work-flow charts and relationship charts have been developed, the group is ready to finalize the implementation plan.

Before you start

1. ' Make sure the subgroups have finished their work-flow charts and relationship maps for each of their action plans and are prepared to present them to the whole group.

2. Schedule the meeting.

3. Assemble materials, including a flip chart and markers.

What to do

Steps	Specifics
Conduct the second implementation planning meeting. Follow the steps below.	
1. Have subgroups present their work-flow charts and relationship maps for their action plans.	
2. Sequence the action plans.	Let them know that action plans can run concurrently if it's workable to do so.
3. Have the group create a preliminary schedule of end dates for each action plan.	
4. Develop preliminary time lines and list the resources needed.	Reassemble the subgroups. Ask subgroups to • Create preliminary time lines for their action plans based on the end dates that the entire group established • List the resources needed to complete each task in their plan, including labor, equipment, and budget needs

Steps	Specifics
5. Select a project manager to oversee each plan.	Ask the group's manager to either get a volunteer project manager for each plan or assign each plan to the group member who's best able to manage that type of change.
6. Identify vulnerable areas in the above plans.	Reassemble as a large group. Ask the group to identify • Problems that could occur in each vulnerable area • The most likely cause of each problem • Actions to prevent each problem • Actions to minimize each problem's effects
7. Identify and add actions to prevent anticipated problems.	
8. Plan periodic maintenance meetings.	The meetings will allow the group to • Celebrate milestones and successes • Share lessons learned • Troubleshoot problems

Exhibit 9.2 shows this procedure.

Exhibit 9.2 Second Implementation Meeting

Steps	Description	Comments
1	Subgroups present work-flow charts and relationship for action plans. (Subgroups)	Review of action plans.
2	Sequence action plans. (Team)	Specify plans that could run concurrently.
3	Create preliminary schedule of end dates for each action plan. (Team)	
4	Develop preliminary time lines and list needed resources. (Subgroups)	Subgroups meet to set time lines and list resources.
5	Select project managers. (Marty and Team)	Ask for volunteers. Qualify according to ability and skills.
6	Identify vulnerable areas in plans. (Team)	Identify: • Problems that could come up in each area. • Most likely causes for problems. • Preventive measures. • Actions to minimize problems' effects.
7	Categorize and add problem prevention to action plans. (Team)	Consolidate similar problems, decide what should be done, and add to plans.
8	Plan periodic maintenance meetings. (Marty and Team)	Agenda for meetings: • Celebrate progress and successes. • Share lessons learned. • Troubleshoot problems.

Implement and Consolidate the New System

Purpose of this procedure

Lawrence Miller (1991) points out that "it is almost impossible to come up with a perfect design — on paper! Only when you begin to implement will you learn how the design needs to be modified" (p. 209).

When you read about implementation, it sounds pretty straightforward. You simply execute your plan. When you actually implement a new process, however, it's never that easy. That's because implementation entails an action-learning process, in which the work group continuously tries out and fine-tunes the new system. This action learning results in a self-renewing system that continuously assesses, interprets, and adapts itself.

As Beer, Eisenstat, and Spector (1990) have pointed out, the implementation process should allow the work group to try out changes informally, before they make permanent changes. It should allow team members to adjust to new roles in a low-risk environment, *before* any new appraisal, compensation, or reward systems apply. Since these kinds of changes often cause anxiety and political resistance, it's a good idea to allow the fledgling system to get on its feet before making them.

After the group installs the new system, the greatest threat is backsliding. Whenever things get comfortable, it's easy for people to slip back into old habits. Whenever the group stops improving the system, both the system and the group will go backwards. To avoid backsliding, the group must hold regular process-improvement forums to

- Celebrate milestones and successes
- Troubleshoot
- Share lessons learned
- Experiment with new ways of working

When to use this procedure

With its planning complete, the group is ready to implement and consolidate the new system. Basically, when the group implements the new system they simply apply the implementation plan developed in the two previous procedures.

Before you start

1. Ask the group to determine which parts of the design specifications are critical to the new system's success and which parts are negotiable. Determine consequences of changing critical parts of the plan. Decide under what circumstances the work group should recommend *not* to proceed.

2. Determine which parts of the plan those who must approve it (probably, at a minimum, the group manager's manager) can and *cannot* live with. List their probable underlying concerns.

3. Consider how the plan would need to change to address these underlying concerns. Negotiate workable changes to the plan, or decide *not* to proceed.

4. Revise the plan as necessary.

5. Ask the work group's manager to review

   - Work and information flows

   - Goals, objectives, and criteria

   - Roles, responsibilities, and relationships

6. Ask the manager to identify help he or she needs in

   - Establishing preliminary expectations and criteria for the work group's performance

   - Coaching work group members in how to define a project's critical path, milestones, and measures; schedule tasks; and budget and allocate resources

   - Facilitating group processes, including planning, decision making, problem solving, and conflict resolution

   - Coordinating efforts across groups

   - Managing integration of new members and reassignments (loss) of old members

   - Managing emotional responses to each stage of the change process

   - Strategizing responses to changes in internal politics, technology, the competitive or regulatory environments, or the labor force

7. Provide the work group's manager with the job aids, training, and tools he or she needs to assume his or her new role.

8. Ask work group members to review:

   - Work and information flows

   - Goals, objectives, and criteria

   - Roles, responsibilities, and relationships

9. Ask group members to identify help they need in

   - Performing essential technical tasks (including operational and troubleshooting tasks)

   - Gathering and interpreting information about customer requirements and external demands, conformance to end- and interim-product measures, and system performance

   - Expediting information flow

   - Making data-based decisions, solving problems, and negotiating resolutions as a group

   - Planning, contributing to, and evaluating group meetings

What to do

Steps	Specifics
1. Based on needs identified, provide job aids, training, or tools.	Meet the specific needs of the manager and the individual work group members identified in the *Before you start* section.
2. Have the work group informally try out the new system (without formal changes in job assignments or appraisal and reward systems).	Expect a temporary *decline* in performance as the work group learns the new system.
3. Conduct an interim assessment of the tryout.	Facilitate a meeting to discuss these questions: • Is the design producing the desired performance and quality of work life? • How well does the group's structure support the work process? • Is the design still appropriate to the environment?
4. Facilitate weekly or biweekly operations and trouble-shooting meetings.	These meetings should apply a systematic problem-solving process to • Define problem(s). • Locate causes • Set solution criteria • Generate a range of possible solutions • Select appropriate solutions based on criteria • Plan and assign action steps for implementing solutions
5. Make periodic, systematic reassessments of the design's effectiveness, efficiency, appropriateness, and adaptability.	Ideally, these should occur every three to six months.

(continued on next page)

Steps	Specifics

6. Adapt the design and take actions as necessary to minimize problems that arise in implementation.

7. Make official reassignments of work group members.

8. Make the changes to appraisal systems.

9. Make the changes to the compensation and reward systems.

10. Make the official changes to the organizational structure (and corresponding organizational chart) that reflect the new system. | Communicate the change and celebrate the accomplishment.

The job is done . . . for the time being.

Exhibit 9.3 shows a flowchart of how the tryout might be assessed.

Exhibit 9.3   Tryout Assessment

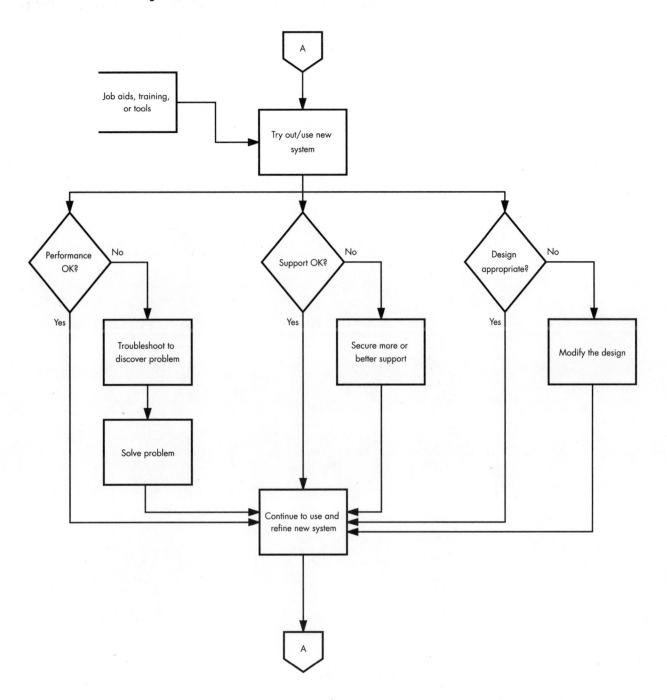

WORK PROCESS REDESIGN IN ACTION

Overview

What is this section about?

The procedures in this book offer guidelines for designing functional work processes — nothing more, nothing less. They're guidelines, period. As such, you are strongly encouraged to modify them, improve them, use them in your own way to meet your own particular needs. That's what the people in this case study did.

The case study in this section shows you how one work group, in one company, with the leadership of one person, used the guidelines in this book to improve its work process. Not all of the procedures in the book were used. Yet, many of them were. Those that were used were modified to fit the situation; to allow success to happen.

CHAPTER 10

From Full Warehouse to Just-in-Time: Case Study of Redesigning the Brandon Companies Distribution Department

The Brandon Companies, Inc., has five large furniture and accessory outlets in a midsized metropolitan area in the Midwest. In addition, they have a mail-order operation, a large furniture repair and refinishing shop, a used furniture outlet, and an auction house that specializes in estate sales. All the businesses are controlled by the Brandon family through a closely held corporate structure.

Until recently their emphasis has been on discounting. The company bought in train-car lots and made volume discount deals with furniture makers and other suppliers. Although this policy worked well in the 1980s, business volume has declined and the company is no longer making the kind of profit it wants. Warehousing and distribution are particularly expensive and are becoming more of a burden.

The company has decided on three major changes. The first is to change its marketing emphasis. The decision is to keep all assets in place, but to move away from discounting toward top quality and customer service. The first move in this direction is a five-year warranty on all merchandise for any defect not attributable to normal wear and tear.

The second move is to reengineer the corporate management structure. Personnel functions for all corporate elements will be consolidated and moved to one place. The training function will also be centralized, with two ramifications: the first is a mandate to certify all instructors in clerical sales and customer relations; the second is to make Training directly responsible for developing needed skills for every job category in the company, including executive management.

The third strategic change is to incorporate just-in-time supply. Brandon has begun to set up arrangements with large-volume suppliers to ship directly from the factory to customers when possible and to reduce warehousing operations by at least a third by the end of this fiscal year. These moves require guaranteeing minimum volumes from some suppliers and agreeing to smaller margins with others. In addition, Brandon will do more to ensure quality by inspecting inventory at the factory. Customers will be alerted to demand a Brandon Seal of Quality on each piece of merchandise they buy.

Distribution will change drastically. Currently distribution is primarily a warehousing operation. Goods and merchandise arrive at disbursement points — usually the stores where they will be retailed — and are uncrated, inspected, and put in storage. They are moved into display areas on demand. For some stores this requires a 200-percent overstock on many items. To accommodate this huge inventory, Brandon has one of the largest warehouse operations in the Midwest. Inventory is accumulated in the main warehouse. It's moved from there to a distribution center. From the distribution center it goes to retail (or other) locations for disbursement. Current plans are to sell the warehouse (within two years) and handle all merchandise through the distribution center.

Mary Rickover and her people in Distribution have been given the mandate to make the change. They know they need help, so they have hired a consulting firm, Change Consultants, to provide advice and expertise. Mary is determined to involve her people as much as possible and to do what needs to be done internally. She has met with her managers and supervisors and has given them three immediate goals:

1. Document your work group's current responsibilities—what it does for Brandon and how that relates to the company now. Basically, what impact do you have on Brandon's current ability to make a profit? Be sure to consider your operation in terms of the big picture, even to the extent of your group's impact on the environment and society.

2. Analyze your functions. How is work accomplished? Who does what? For what kinds of reasons? What do you produce? For what customers (both internal and external)?

3. Consider what you *must* change to accommodate the new mission and vision. What other kinds of changes might be profitable? When should work process changes begin? When should they be in place?

Let's see how her decisions might affect one of her work groups. The work group is currently called Transportation. Their basic responsibility is to move merchandise from the point of delivery to the warehouse or distribution center and from facility to facility within the company. They are also responsible for the security of the merchandise in transit and for recycling materials used to pack merchandise during shipment.

Jim Kelly is Manager of Transportation. He has been with Brandon for seventeen years. All of his experience is connected with moving merchandise around. He started as a stocker in one of the stores. Jim has three supervisors reporting directly to him: Mike Cernisky is in charge of large-volume operations such as unloading freight cars (when it's necessary) and moving inventory from the warehouse to the distribution center; Judy Cavanaugh handles forklift and small-volume moves; Juan Perdido coordinates the work. He distributes workers, handles staffing problems, and keeps track of other personnel problems or situations.

Jim has thought about the nature of the changes he and his people face. They could lead to a major shake-up of his operation; but he isn't sure how, or what the ramifications might be. One thing he is sure of — if some serious planning doesn't happen quickly, his whole department could bog down into chaos. He asks Mary for a little advice and whatever help she can offer.

Mary arranges for one of the people from Change Consultants to work directly with Jim and his people. Change Consultants assigns Manny McBee, who has three years' experience working on reengineering projects. Her father works for Yellow Freight as an expeditor.

Jim and Manny meet with Mike, Judy, and Juan to try to work out the situation, to define desired outcomes for Brandon's transportation department. They spend a Saturday working through the procedure. When they finally quit at about 9 P.M., they have a feeling they have accomplished something worthwhile. Manny tells them he will work over his notes and bring them a draft of the results of the session Tuesday morning.

On Tuesday Manny meets with the team again to go over his outcomes from Saturday's session. He tells them, "Here's what I think I heard you say," and gives them each a copy of a completed desired outcomes worksheet.

Desired Outcomes Worksheet

Items	*Outcomes*
Anticipated process results	1. Eliminate need to move goods to warehouse.
	2. Reduce damage to merchandise caused by internal workers by 80%.
	3. Delivery of merchandise from external supplier within 48 hours.
	4. Delivery from internal locations within 2 hours.
	5. Reduce time in process for paperwork by at least 50%.
	6. Reduce overtime pay by at least 50%.
	7. Reduce downtime for equipment (trucks, forklifts, and conveyors) by 20%.
	8. Improve ratio of recycled waste materials to as close to 100% as possible; 96% seems reasonable.
	9. Reduce shrinkage to less than 1%.
	10. Provide dependable documentation of merchandise locations for primary and secondary storage and a way to trace goods in tertiary locations.
	11. Decrease reliance on temporary labor by at least 80%.
	12. Move responsibility for work results to the workers.
Business results	1. Reduce cost of transportation to Brandon Company by 32% within two years.
	2. Improve customer appreciation of the company by providing on-time delivery of unsullied goods.

Items	Outcomes

Customer groups	1. Internal:
	• Distribution center
	• Main retail outlets
	• Catalogue store
	• Used furniture outlet
	• Refinishing and fabrication centers
	• Company headquarters
	2. External:
	• Current
	  —Recyclers
	  —Special order or special request (emergencies or expedited)
	• Future(?)
	  —Individual buyers
	  —Subdivision developers
	  —Interior designers, residential
	  —Interior designers, business
	  —Government agencies

Product or services provided to each group	1. General: Load, transport, unload, place in storage.
	2. Internal:
	  — Just-in-time delivery
	  — Prompt pick-up
	  — Zero damage to merchandise
	  — Courteous, friendly partnering
	3. External:
	  — Delivery within one-half hour of promised time
	  — Hassle free, courteous, and flexible
	  — Paperwork and documentation accurate and free of undue complications

Customer requirements	1. On-time delivery of the specific item(s) requested 2. Undamaged merchandise 3. Cost at or below independent suppliers 4. Availability on demand

(continued on next page)

Desired Outcomes Worksheet *(cont.)*

Items	Outcomes
Competitive advantages	1. Time in process — competitors take more time to schedule and have longer delay up front. 2. Responsiveness — can respond in minutes. 3. Costs less per item delivered.
Performance indicators	See above.
Levels of indicators	See above.
Suppliers	1. Rail (merchandise). Burlington. 2. Overland trucker, large company (merchandise). Preston and Hunt. 3. Overland trucker, independent (merchandise). Jerry Burns, Kathy Cronkite. 4. Furniture company vans and trucks (merchandise). Caravan, La-Z-Boy, Walnut Creations. 5. Capital equipment — trucks, forklifts, etc. Harvester, Ford. 6. Parts and supplies. Gem Distributors, AMP, Mertz, Firestone. 7. Recycler. Greenbelt. 8. Labor. Temps, Inc.
Inputs from suppliers	1. Merchandise. 2. Equipment. Trucks, vans, forklifts (three purposes), conveyors, hand tools. 3. Parts and supplies. 4. Labor. Drivers, pickers and loaders, clerical, general labor, and sometimes supervisory.
Requirements for inputs	To be determined by each manager.
Internal quality of work life	For this operation, workers are fairly content with conditions. Workplaces are clean and well arranged. Workers seem to respond well to supervisors (with one or two exceptions). However, the weather and the tendency for customers to be demanding can cause problems.
Adaptability	Reason for this study. Must be increased. Nature and complexity of work will change considerably within the next twelve months.
Complexity	Not much of a concern at this point. Computerization is handled by other departments. Will have some problems with LORAN system and use of barcoding on merchandise packaging. Don't anticipate a big change in type or operation of equipment in the near future.

Items	Outcomes
Interdependencies	Not a problem at this time. Unit is fairly autonomous except for relationships with internal customers and overhead.
Growth needs?	None. In fact we expect a gradual reduction in staffing needs.
Reconciliation of group wants and requirements	Incompatibilities: 1. Group members want to be in line for promotion, but at present there is no access to jobs outside Transportation. 2. Company movement toward more education in new hires doesn't jibe with workers' perceptions of need. 3. Many workers want to use Spanish on the job, and don't like to have to speak to each other in English in ordinary conversations. 4. Drivers aren't pleased with having to learn and use LORAN system. 5. There is some concern that people will be laid off.
Comparison of results with what was expected	Not prepared to do this at this time; delay until more information is in hand about new ways of doing things.

The group studies the sheets and compares the results with their own notes. Then they have a short discussion of the results and what they mean. Manny lets them talk for several minutes before saying, "This, as far as I can tell at this time, is a very good start. We now have direction and can begin to think about how to get from here to there. The next step is to support these findings with more information, more detail."

"So, how do we go about that?" a member asks.

"The best way is to simply ask people who know the answers." Manny pauses. "Before we start, though, I think it would be a good idea to organize our effort so we don't waste time or energy." At their nods he continues, "Here's a matrix that provides some insight into who we should talk to about what."

Preliminary Assessment Matrix

Activity	Manager	Work Group	Suppliers	Customers
Compare actual results to planned results	Primary source	Secondary source		
Estimate customer requirements	Secondary source			Primary source
Compare current products/services to customer requirements				Primary source
Identify requirements for suppliers	Secondary source	Primary source		
Judge quality of supplier inputs		Primary source	Secondary source	
Specify current work conditions (quality of work life)	Secondary source	Primary source		
List anticipated work conditions (quality of work life)	Primary source	Secondary source		
Determine gaps between current and anticipated quality of work life	Primary source	Secondary source		
List other process-related problems and anticipated problems	Primary source	Primary source	Secondary source	Secondary source

They discuss the table and who to talk to about each category. After a while Jim takes the lead and suggests which of them might interview whom and how to organize the effort. They agree to take a week to prepare the interviews, conduct them, and assemble the results. Once they have all seen the results and considered them they will meet again to work on the next step, comparing what is with what ought to be.

Jim used the gap verification checklist to prepare for the meeting. A sample of Jim's work follows.

Gap Verification Checklist

Step	Description	Date	Comments
1	Explain list of gaps (probable problems) to manager.		1. Two major cost areas — people and equipment. One or both must be cut to achieve cost goals. 2. It may be difficult to get retail managers to use new system. 3. Just-in-time will require more staff. 4. Drivers and roustabouts may feel threatened as well as stuck in dead-end jobs.
2	Revise to reflect manager's input.		1. Executive expects to modernize equipment, double capital budget for two years. 2. Retail guys know they will benefit — expect total cooperation. 3. Shouldn't need more people — use present staff differently, firefighter model. 4. My problem.

(continued on next page)

Gap Verification Checklist *(cont.)*

Step	Description	Date	Comments
3	Pinpoint the specific elements of the work process that each problem impacts.		1. People have to learn new equipment, especially LORAN. Preventive maintenance becomes even more important. Must get modern diagnostic tools for maintenance workers.
			2. Must set up dialogue with store managers so no one gets unpleasant surprise. Inventory control shared with us. Must develop countershrinkage measures before a problem appears.
			3. This will require a whole new method for responses. Create labor pool, with individuals assigned on an as-needed basis. People and equipment have to be ready to move immediately. Must huddle with union as soon as possible to work out this problem. Scheduling at two levels: A) daily/ordinary, and B) bull pen. Bull pen has priority.
			4. Union can help here, but I will work to make paths available for others.
4	Specify processes that		
	• Are least effective and efficient at producing outcomes		See 3.3 above.
	• Have greatest impact on customer satisfaction.		See 3.2 and 3.3 above.
	• Provide best balance between potential payoff and likelihood of success.		See 3.3 above.

Step	Description	Date	Comments
5	Set objectives for each process named.		1. Preliminary study of vendors and products complete in three months. Ask for bids from top three vendors. Set delivery and payment schedules in six months. Accept first delivery in six months. Eighty percent mark is 18 months, reserve final 20% to supplement original investment. Begin depreciation on day of first delivery (inform bookkeeping). Phase out old equipment by end of 24th month. 2. Dialogues established within two weeks. Informal agreements by first of next month. Formalize at direction of executive management. 3. Define extent and nature of problem. Specify alternatives for meeting challenge. Select best alternative (balance efficiency and effectiveness). Try out. Make changes. Assign staff. Set responsibilities.
6	Identify critical goals for quality of work life		(See 5 above.)
7	Describe design-process tasks.		To be done.
8	Specify design-process roles.		
9	Identify resources.		(Highlight in above information.)
10	Identify constraints.		
11	Review results and set the design process in motion.		

NOTE: Your analysis will probably be very different from what is listed here, but it should exhibit the same kinds of thinking and considerations. Most important, it should provide ample information for the next step.

Jim's most immediate concern was to develop a new process for his people to use to do business. His reasoning was that, without it, people would tend to try to work in the same way as before, and that simply wouldn't work out. The new approach would have to be in place before anything else could be established. It also represented the greatest change from current processes. Therefore, he made it his top priority. (Note: The rest of this case study will concentrate on this one process. However, you must keep in mind that all of the other aspects of the change were also in process. This isn't an isolated event.)

Before starting, Jim found a copy of the general procedure flowchart, enlarged it and tacked it to the main bulletin board. As steps were accomplished, he used a big red marker to check them off. Consequently, everyone in Transportation knew from day to day how the project was going. The next three pages show the flowchart.

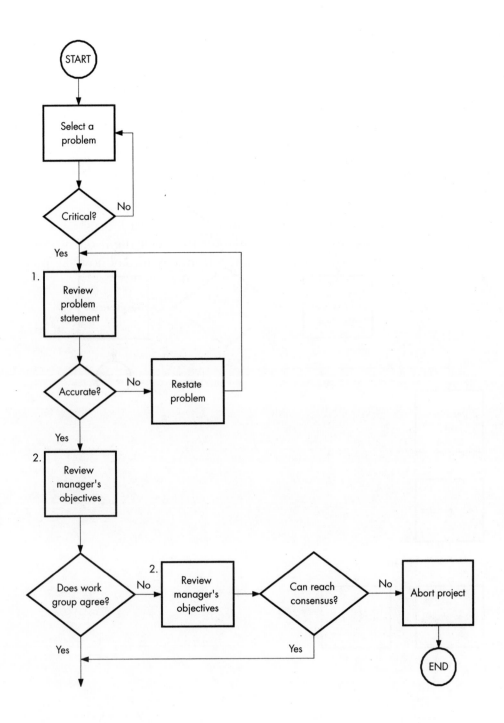

(continued on next page)

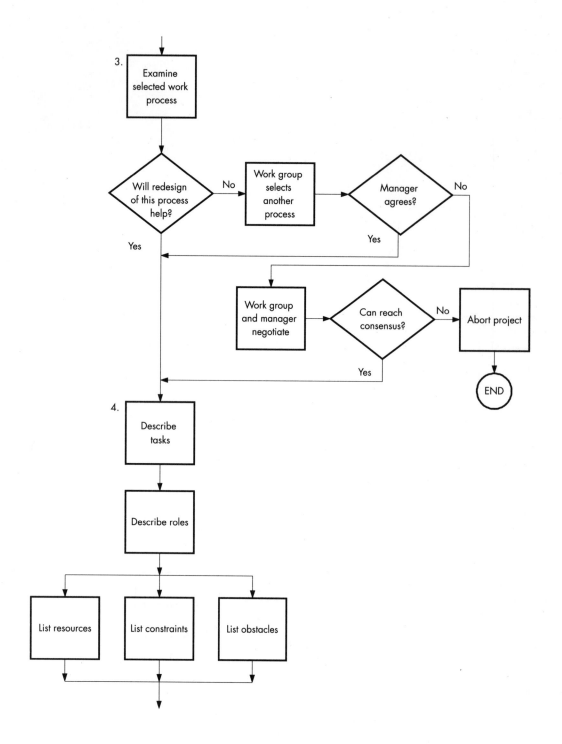

3. Examine selected work process

Will redesign of this process help?

No → Work group selects another process → Manager agrees?

No →

Yes →

Work group and manager negotiate → Can reach consensus?

No → Abort project → END

Yes →

Yes →

4. Describe tasks

Describe roles

List resources   List constraints   List obstacles

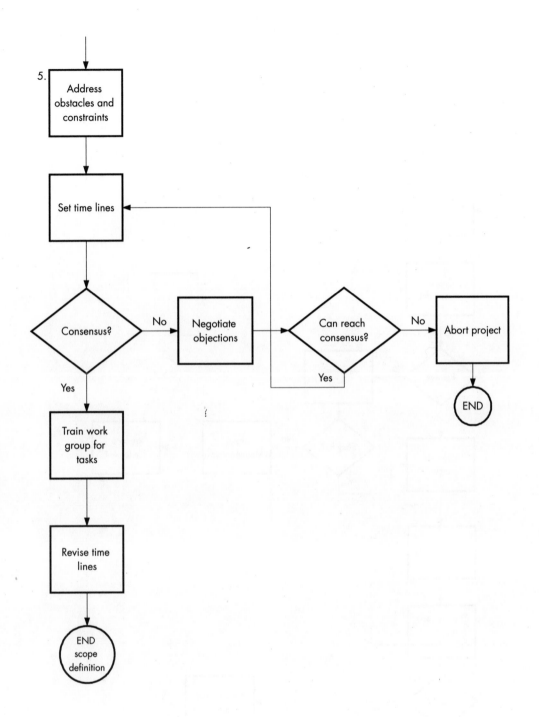

The next task was to develop a work flow for the new process. This is shown here.

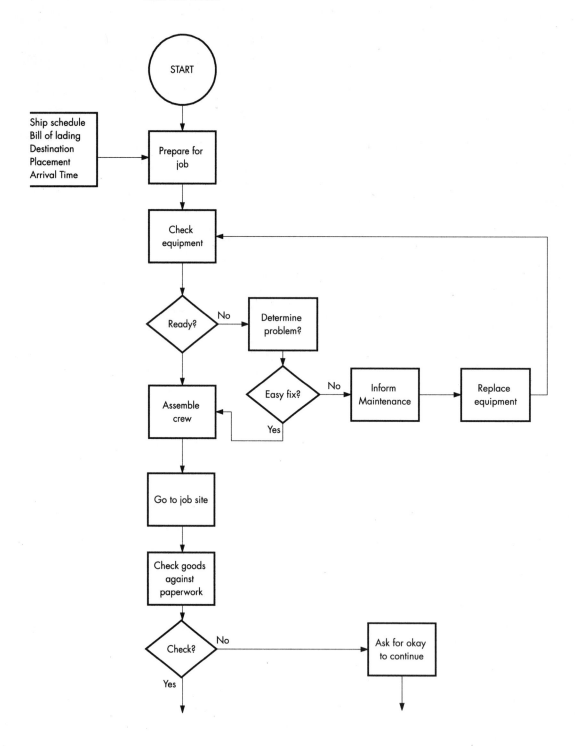

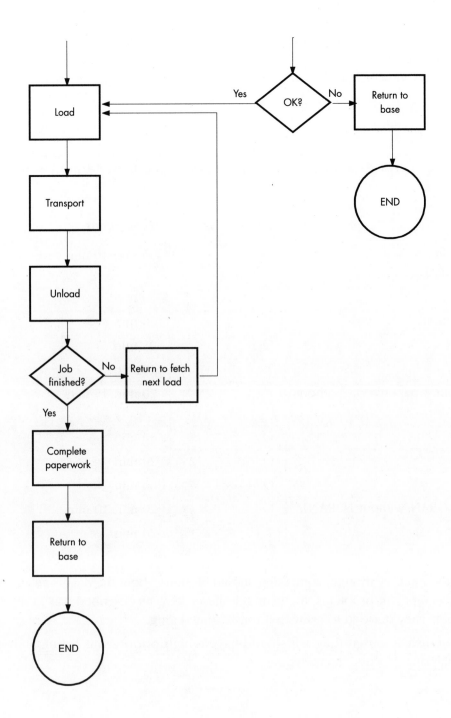

Jim and his work group then began the serious work of developing specifics for the changeover. The first concern was cycle time, since it was the critical element that prompted the change effort in the first place.

Cycle Time Analysis: Transportation, Inventory Movement

Activity	Activity Type	Time Spent
Receive and digest information and specifics about job (without LORAN/with LORAN).	O	45 min/10 min
Check equipment.	I	30 min
Diagnose problems, if appropriate.	D	20 min
Assemble crew.	O	05 min
Go to job site (average).	T	20 min
Check merchandise (etc.) against paperwork (without LORAN/with LORAN).	I	20 min/15 min
Put merchandise on truck.	O	60 min
Transport to destination.	O	20 min
Unload.	O	60 min
Complete paperwork (with LORAN/without LORAN).	O	20 min/10 min
Return to office.	T	20 min

Although they thought something should be done about the delay caused by equipment problems, the team felt the process as described was fairly tight. They decided to go with it for the time being.

The next step that they felt should have a high priority was listing and analyzing process parameters.

Process Parameters Worksheet

Process	Inputs	Outputs	Boundaries	Flow
Prepare for job.	• Shipping schedule. • Bill of lading. • Customer. • Placement of goods at customer site. • Planned arrival time at customer.	• Go/no-go decision. • Specification of equipment to be used.	• Begins as soon as order comes from customer/shipper. • LORAN database must be updated. • Ends with manager okay (can be assumed in most cases) to proceed.	Directly to crew foreman, management, and customer (through LORAN).
Check equipment.	• Available equipment (trucks, loaders, etc.) • Prejob checklist. • Lumber fasteners and glue, and other materials. • Skilled workers. • Equipment and tools.	Decision about which equipment to use for the job.	• Begins as soon as nature of job is known (size of load, number in crew, procedure to be used). • Ends when equipment has been selected and checked.	• Directly to job activity. • Indirectly to maintenance (when problems are encountered, crew can't handle them quickly).
Assemble crew.	• People available. • Skill sets. • Time constraints per individual.	Crew in truck ready to go.	• Begins with initiation of job order. • Ends when truck leaves.	To management, union, and war room.

(continued on next page)

Process Parameters Worksheet *(cont.)*

Process	Inputs	Outputs	Boundaries	Flow
Proceed to job site.	Equipment and crew.	Safe arrival.	• Begins as soon as crew is mounted. • Ends at arrival.	N/A.
Check merchandise against paperwork.	• Goods in current location. • Bill of lading. • LORAN database.	Decision about whether there is a match.	• Begins on arrival. • Ends with final check.	To management and customer through LORAN.
Load.	• Okay to proceed, or • Match from check.	Goods on truck.	• Begins as soon as okay is received or check shows a match. • Ends when truck is loaded.	N/A.
Transport.	Truck loaded.	Goods at customer site.	• Begins as soon as load is certified by foreman. • Ends when truck arrives at customer site.	To management (in case load is partial).
Unload.	Loaded truck at customer site.	Goods placed in locations as previously arranged with customer.	• Begins with arrival at customer site. • Ends when all goods are placed as prescribed.	To management and customer through LORAN.

Process	Inputs	Outputs	Boundaries	Flow
Complete paperwork.	• LORAN procedure. • Bill of lading. • Customer request sheet.	Complete documentation of transport, including time sheets for crew.	• Begins as soon as load is at location. • Ends with acknowledgment from LORAN.	To management and customer through LORAN.
Return to office.	N/A.	• Equipment returned to pool. • Crew returned to pool. • Documents filed in "in box." • LORAN informed of end of job.	• Begins on arrival at office (or en route). • Ends with notification to LORAN.	To management through LORAN and completed forms in "in box." (Forms include dated and initialed bill of lading).

Jim and the department found, as they examined the parameters worksheet, that information flow could be a real problem, particularly if the LORAN system broke down. They decided to rough out an information flow to discover where, if any, real problems might be lurking.

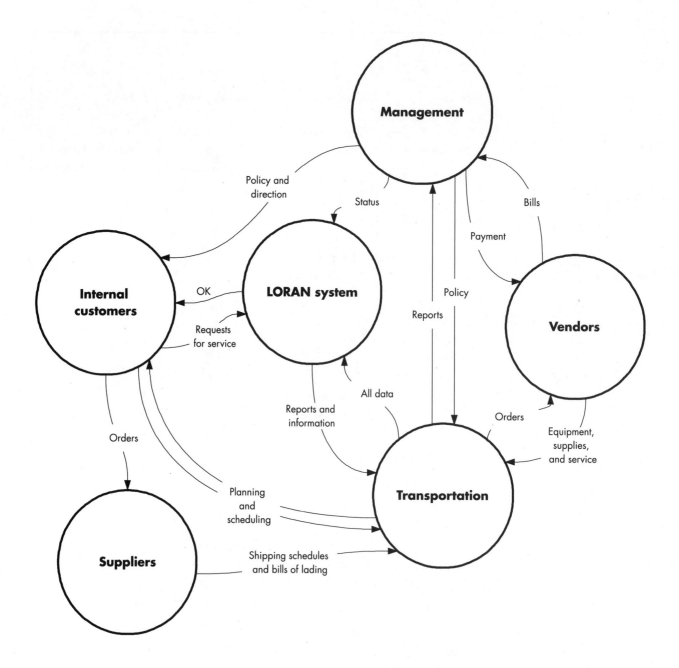

After some discussion the work group decided that information could and would flow well, particularly if they concentrated on establishing good dialogues with retailers and management. The most obvious problem seemed to be the lack of a direct link from retailers back to management. They prepared a memo to executive management outlining their concern. Then they began to study the relationships between all the process functions more closely. A two-person team took the information gathered so far and prepared a relationship map.

RELATIONSHIP MAP
Brandon Transportation Department

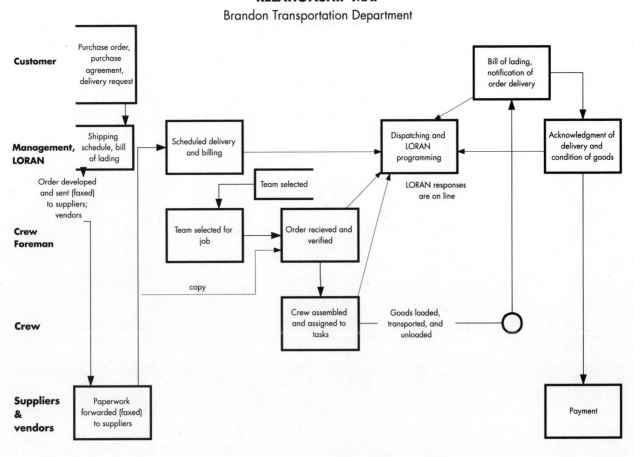

Jim and the task force discussed the need for a variance analysis. They agreed it would be a very valuable tool, but it would be practically impossible to construct because so much of the old way of doing things was going to be discarded. The task force members asked Jim if he thought it would be valuable to develop a variance analysis downstream, perhaps six months along, to check performance against expectations. Jim heartily agreed, and they put the item on the table for six months.

The next step was to develop a simple chart of the process functions and determine who could be made responsible to see that they were completed. The chart was developed as a group exercise with the entire department. Their first reaction was "everybody should be responsible for everything." However, after considerable debate, they broke "everybody" into three groups: the manager (Jim), crew forepersons, and crew members. Jim asked them to add four peripheral groups: executive management, store management, suppliers, and maintenance. The resulting matrix looked like the one on the next page.

Brandon Responsibility Chart—Transportation Department

Activity	Jim	Fore-person	Crew Members	Executive Manage-ment	Store Manage-ment	Suppliers	Mainten-ance
Keep LORAN database up-to-date and accurate.	I	R	I	S	A		
Check equipment.	I	R	R				A/R
Perform diagnosis when equipment malfunctions.	I	R	A				R
Assemble crew.	A	R		I			
Go to job site.	A	R	R	I	I	I	
Check manifest.	I	R	S			A	
Load.		R	R		I	A	
Transport.		A	R		I	I	
Unload.	I	R	R		A	I	
Return.	I	R	R				
Develop bids for equipment replacement.	R	S	I	S/A		I	R
Input shipping schedules and data from bills of lading to LORAN.		R	A		R		
Meet with retail managers to plan and schedule.	R	I	I	I/A	R		I
Prepare reports to management.	R	S	I	A	I		

R   =   Is *responsible* for doing the step or making the decision
A   =   Must *approve* the step or decision
S   =   Must *support* the step or decision with resources
I   =   Must be *informed* of the step or decision
Blank =   Doesn't contribute directly to the step or decision

So even though the work group was unable to come up with a variance analysis, they could and did outline a general scheme for spotting variances and taking care of them.

At their next meeting, Jim could sense a heightened sense of optimism in the group. They were beginning to believe they could do this. One of the problems remaining had to do with scheduling more or less regular runs, such as trips to pick up merchandise for refurbishing. Two of the drivers, Mary and Martin, brought in a map of the city with Brandon locations circled on it. Then they showed the group a diagram they developed to show work flow.

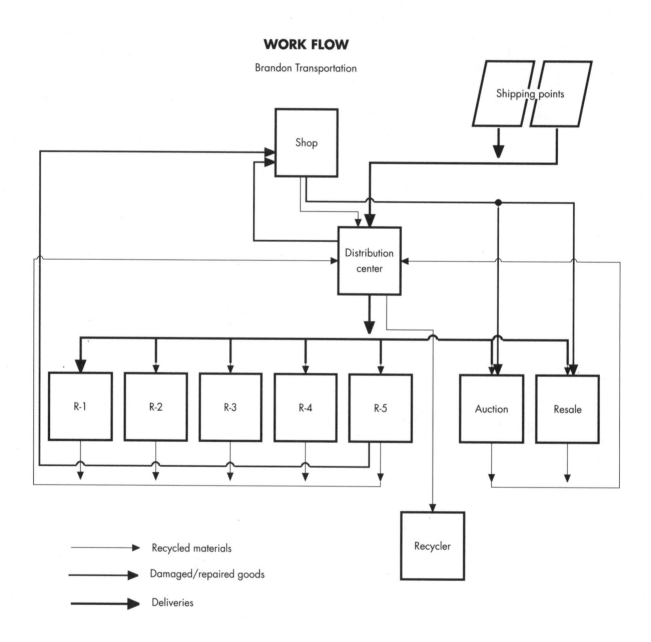

WORK FLOW

Brandon Transportation

The work-flow chart showed what seemed to be duplication of effort. Each store was visited at least twice per day: once for deliveries from shipping points and once to pick up recyclable packing materials. In addition there were trips about once per week from the repair shop to each retail store for pickups and an equal number of trips to the resale store with newly reconditioned merchandise.

The amount of effort used to recycle seemed inordinate. As the group discussed it, two alternatives came out: 1) they could continue as before and make an effort to reduce the number of trips needed, or 2) they could outsource the pickups to the recycling company. The drawback to the second alternative was that they would lose the revenue they presently earned from recycling. Since the group couldn't make an informed decision at the time, they appointed Mary and Martin to develop a simple cost-versus-benefit analysis of the recycling effort.

Jim and the group next decided it was time to move on to the next set of tasks: defining and describing their jobs. The first step was easy. They decided the new (changed) department would have two kinds of jobs: the manager and everybody else. Although someone would have to provide leadership in certain situations, they didn't see why such a person would need a special title. After all, different people provided leadership in different situations.

During the next week, while different small groups worked on the several tasks, Jim met with union representatives to reach an agreement that would allow the work group to do as it planned. The union representative compromised by giving them eighteen months as a trial period. He asked for the right to negotiate with management when the trial period was over. Jim presented the plan to management and they agreed — if the negotiations began with a redefinition of the job category.

Much relieved, Jim focused again on the changeover. First he reviewed the task/skill matrix developed by his task force (partially reproduced on the following pages).

Task/Skill Matrix

New Job: Cartage Specialist.

Defined: A cartage specialist is a person within the Transportation Department who is responsible for pickup, transportation, and delivery of merchandise and other items as requested by internal customers.

Task	Skills	Resources	Outcomes
Understand and use "request for service."	Basic education.	Shipping orders, bills of lading, shipping schedules, store manager request forms, and LORAN.	All service requests and ship orders are interpreted on time and accurately.
Operate trucks and other equipment safely and efficiently.	Driving. Other skills as needed depending on the equipment.	The equipment. Books and operating manuals. Training offered internally and by vendors.	Equipment is operated safely and with professional expertise.
Perform preventive maintenance on commonly used equipment.	Ability to locate specific parts and places and adjust, clean, and make simple repairs.	Specified tools, cleaning materials, and manuals.	Equipment operates at maximum efficiency and effectiveness with less than 5% downtime.
Diagnose the cause of problems with equipment.	Ability to use the manual to locate and specify the nature of a problem with • A 2½-ton truck. • A utility van. • A semi-tractor/ trailer. • A front loader and forklift.	Manual, Sun diagnostic equipment, and vendor rep (as needed).	Problems beyond those found in the afternoon are diagnosed without delay so repair or replacement can take place within 24 hours.

Task	Skills	Resources	Outcomes
Load/unload goods.	Operate forklift and hand truck. Use safe procedures for lifting and moving goods. Locate and secure goods within truck and at destination.	Equipment (see above).	Goods are moved safely and quickly. They are located as expected by customer. Damage to merchandise less than 5% of the time. No shrinkage.
Operate LORAN equipment.	Able to key-in data and bring up cost figures, location information, and special customer requirements.	LORAN system, operating manual, and training.	Eighty percent of paperwork is replaced by LORAN functions.

Attribute	Business Purpose	Forces That Influence Performance	Business Gain from Good Performance
Skilled team of two available at all business hours.	1. Facilitate "just-in-time" stocking of merchandise. 2. Avoid necessity to store goods in warehouse. 3. Reduce storage costs levied by shippers.	Size of staff (has to be large enough so one team can be on call at all times). Training and experience (team must perform to standards).	Eliminate need for warehouse. Quality service to retail stores.
Top-quality preventive maintenance.	1. Reduce amount of time equipment is down. 2. Reduce maintenance costs.	Size of staff. Diagnostic skills.	Reduced maintenance costs. Longer service time for equipment. More employee satisfaction.

Then Jim went over some of the attributes of the job with his task force.

As he looked at these things, Jim noted some characteristics his workers would have to have. For example, their vision would have to be correctable to 20/20 and they would have to be able to lift thirty pounds without strain. While he was thinking about it, he scribbled out a list of other proposed requirements for people applying for the new job. He would discuss them with the whole department at the next meeting:

Application Criteria for Cartage Specialist:

1. Must easily learn to read and understand shipping schedules, bills of lading, etc.

2. Must be physically able to key-in data on the LORAN (i.e., it would be very difficult for a one-armed person).

3. Candidates must have

   - A valid Class A driver's license (standard passenger car)

   - No DWIs or DUIs in the last five years

   - No record of reckless driving or more than two speeding tickets in the past two years

4. Candidates should

   - Have the capacity to accept criticism from customers without undue emotional stress

   - Be able to document and develop a report for normal operations activity

   - Be able to troubleshoot mechanical problems

Then Jim developed a sample matrix showing how one of his current workers (on the job for three months) stacked up.

Summary for Jason Jackson

Skill Area	Extent in Hand	Gap	How to Remedy
Use documents	Medium	Not large	Continue to work with them; ask partner (Max) questions; come to me when stumped.
Keying skills	High	Small to none	N/A
Driving skills/record	High	Small to none	(This guy is very good, may be able to use him as tutor for new hires.)
Accept criticism	Low	Very large	Lets temper show at times, alienates customers. Special seminar or workshop.
Document and report	Medium	Not large	Keep practicing under Max's direction.
Troubleshoot	High	Small	(Seems to take to it well.) Introduce him to more types of equipment.

The next department meeting was full of fun and goodwill. As it neared conclusion the group roughed out an action plan. See next page.

Action Plan for Brandon Transportation

All steps except the final presentation are the responsibility of the task force.

Step	Description	Results	Planned Dates	Actual Date
1. Initiate.	Assemble team, decide which team members will be responsible for each activity. Finalize budget and assign resources. Develop review process and feedback mechanisms.	Budget and review process, team roster, and assigned roles.	2/28–3/4	
2. Research.	Contact other organizations and search the literature for descriptions of similar work flows, why they were adopted, and what effect they have had on productivity.	General description of the new process.	3/7–3/25	
3. Develop preliminary description of the process.	Prepare preliminary description of how work will be done. Include as much detail as possible.	Full description of work flow with each task explained in detail.	3/28–4/22	
4. Brainstorm	Discuss the process. Answer these questions: • How will it fit in with current company operations? • What elements are not necessary? • What should be added? • What are the basic requirements for budgeting and assignment of resources? • What skills do we have in hand? • What additional skills should we have to get a good start?	Modifications to process.	4/30 (Sat.)	
5. Develop final version.	Format according to company policy and present to executive management.	Final, formal version of intended process.	5/2–5/5	

The room was slightly stuffy because the hotel had only recently turned on its air conditioning. Jim sipped a glass of water as he watched the "Brandon Family" file in and take seats. They had all had time to read the report, but he was unsure about whether they had actually taken the time to digest it and consider its implications for the company. He wiped a sweaty palm on his new suit and adjusted his tie for the hundredth time. Then he glanced again to his boss, Mary Rickover. Her smile was dazzling. "Piece of cake," she said.

"Hunh?"

"It's a piece of cake, Jim. You've done an excellent job with this. I doubt if any other department has done as well. So relax."

And he did. Her words had the right kind of effect. He waited for the usual table chatter to quiet, and began. Twenty minutes later, he turned the last page of the report and asked for questions.

"It looks to me like you'll need more staff?" It was Harry from Accounting.

"That's probably true unless we outsource the recycling program, in which case we may be able to cut two or three people. But I'm not sure it's wise to think of cutting staff at this point. We simply don't know enough yet and I feel we must be able to support the just-in-time idea."

William in Personnel nodded and changed the subject. "Are we still on good terms with the union on this?"

"So far, and I don't expect any problems as long as we hold to our schedule."

Mr. Brandon stood abruptly and motioned for Jim to seat himself. When Jim did so, the CEO looked carefully around the table before speaking. "This looks good to me." He thumped the report open before him. "I suggest we give this young man and his 'Cartage Specialists' a chance to make it work, unless any of you see some serious flaw."

Mary spoke up. "Not a serious flaw, sir, but I believe I should share something before you finalize this."

"Go ahead, Mary."

"Well, Sir, the point isn't made in the report, but this will do two important things for my department that aren't directly connected to Transportation. First, it will eliminate the need for our warehouse a full year before you asked. That will save us several hundred thousand dollars. Second, it will make it possible for the rest of Distribution to cut back on staff — not a lot, but enough, I think, to underwrite the whole program."

"You're sure?"

"Fairly — I worked the math through last night."

The old man beamed. He looked around comfortably at the rest of his officers. They were good people, people he knew would speak up if they felt anything should be said. "Are we agreed, then?" At their nods he turned to Jim. "Okay, Mr. Kelly, get on with it."

And he did.

SECTION FOUR

RESOURCES

Overview

This section provides various tools and techniques to assist you in work group and job design interventions. These resources can be used as job aids to guide you through various procedures in this book.

When to use this section

You will want to use this section whenever a procedure refers to a particular resource. Directions for using the resources have been provided to make them user-friendly. You can photocopy them directly, or copy them by hand onto flip chart paper to ease their completion when working in group settings. You may also want to modify them, depending on the specifics of your work group or job design situations.

Resource A   Business Environment Matrix

Directions: In the left column, heading the rows, list influential groups or forces such as customer groups, suppliers, and regulators (including internal auditors, quality control inspectors, etc.).

For each influential group or force, fill in the information requested

- What they expect
- What they provide
- Goals and objectives the work group must set to meet the expectations of the external groups.

External Group/Force	What They Expect	What They Provide	Goals (Current and Future)
1			
2			
3			
4			
5			
6			
7			
8			

Resource B Cycle Time Analysis Worksheet

Purpose: To analyze the things that make up a product's or service's cycle time. This allows you to spot non–value adding activities and delays. (To improve cycle time, eliminate or reduce these things.)

Directions: Follow a product or service through its cycle, from the time you receive the first inputs to the time you deliver it to its customer. Then fill out the worksheet on the following page.

1. In the left column, list where the product or service spends time. Be sure to include all steps, inspections, queues, and delays.

2. In the second column, categorize each item listed in the left column by type.

To represent:	*Write the letter:*
Operations — Altering the characteristics of materials or changing information.	O
Transportation — Moving materials or information from place to place by people or machines.	T
Storage — Storing materials or information before or after use.	S
Inspection — Checking materials or information to determine content, volume, or characteristics.	I
Rework — Re-altering materials or information after the initial operation.	R
Delays — Periods of no operations due to lack of materials or information.	D

3. In the third column, record the amount of time the product is occupied with that item. (Use a single consistent unit of time, such as minutes, hours, days, weeks, etc.)

4. To get the: Do this calculation:

   Total cycle time   Add all listed times

   Total value-adding time   Add all times categorized "O"

   Total non–value adding time   Add all times categorized anything *except* "O"

   Percentage of total cycle time   Divide the total non–value
   spent on non–value   adding time by the total cycle
   adding activity   time

(continued on next page)

Cycle Time Analysis Worksheet *(cont.)*

Activity		Activity Type	Time Spent
1			
2			
3			
4			
5			
6			
7			
8			
9			
10			
11			
12			
13			
14			
15			
16			
17			
18			
19			
20			
21			
22			
23			
24			
25			
26			
27			

Total cycle time _____

Total value-adding time _____

Total non–value adding time _____

Percentage of cycle time spent on non–value adding activity _____

Resource C   *Variance Analysis Worksheet*

Purpose: To describe problems and their causes; also to locate where each problem becomes apparent and gets fixed, and identify who controls its occurrence.

Variance	Cause	Where found?	Where fixed?	Who controls its occurrence?
1				
2				
3				
4				
5				
6				
7				
8				

Resource D   Responsibility Chart

(Originally conceived by Beckhard and Harris [1987])

Purpose: To point out divisions between responsibility and authority and between doing and decision making.

Directions:

1. In the left column, list the steps and decisions required to produce the work group's output.

2. Heading each of the remaining columns, write the name of a work group member or manager.

3. To fill in the cells, record the role that each contributor plays in each step or decision.

If the contributor:	Fill in the cell with an:
Is *responsible* for doing the step or making the decision	R
Must *approve* the step or decision	A
Must *support* the step or decision with resources	S
Must be *informed* of the step or decision	I
Is *irrelevant* to the step or decision	—

4. Highlight problems with the current distribution of responsibility. The following things may indicate a problem:

• More than one R for a single step or decision

• Multiple approvals (As) for a single step or decision

• Barriers between the responsible person (R) and those who must approve (A)

Steps or Decisions	Name 1 _____	Name 2 _____	Name 3 _____	Name 4 _____	Name 5 _____
1					
2					
3					
4					
5					
6					
7					

Resource E Skills and Incentives Matrix

Purpose: To identify the skills required to complete a work process; to determine which of these skills the work group currently has and what happens when they use it.

Directions:

1. In the left column, list the steps of the work process.

2. In the next column to the right, list the skills it takes to do that step successfully.

3. For each skill, answer the questions by marking an "X" in the answer column.

Process/Step	Skills Required	Does the current work group have the skill?		What happens when someone uses the skill?	
		Yes	No	Rewarded	Punished
1					
2					
3					
4					
5					
6					
7					

References

Adizes, I. *Corporate Lifecycles*. Prentice Hall, 1988.

Brandt, S. *Entrepreneuring: Ten Commandments for Building a Growth Company*. Mentor: New American Library, 1982.

Chang, R. Y. "Continuous Process Improvement," the October 1992 issue of *Info-Line* (by the American Society of Training and Development).

Churchill, N. and Lewis, V. "The Five Stages of Small Business Growth," in the May–June, 1983 issue of *Harvard Business Review*.

Cunningham, B. and Eberle, T. "A Guide to Job Enrichment and Redesign" in the February, 1990 issue of *Personnel*.

Davenport, T. *Process Innovation*. Harvard Business School Press, 1993.

Davidow, W. and Uttal, B. *Total Customer Service: The Ultimate Weapon*. Harper Perennial, 1989.

Galbraith, J. R. *Organization Design*. Addison-Wesley, 1977.

Goal/QPC. *The Memory Jogger: A Pocket Guide of Tools for Continuous Improvement*. Goal/QPC, 1988.

Hackman, J. R. and Oldham, G. R. *Work Redesign*. Addison-Wesley, 1980.

Hammer, M. "Reengineering Work: Don't Automate, Obliterate," in the July–August, 1990 issue of *Harvard Business Review*.

Hanna, D. P. *Designing Organizations for High Performance*. Addison-Wesley, 1988.

Harbour, J. L. "Improving Work Processes," in the February 1993 issue of *Performance and Instruction*.

Harrington, H. J. *Business Process Improvement*. McGraw Hill, 1991.

Lawler, E. E. *The Ultimate Advantage*. Jossey-Bass, 1992.

Lynch, R. and Cross, K. *Measure Up! Yardsticks for Continuous Improvement*. Blackwell Business, 1991.

Lytle, W. O. *Socio-Technical Systems Analysis and Design Guide for Linear Work*. Block Petrella Weisbord, 1991.

Lytle, W. O. *Socio-Technical Systems Analysis and Design Guide for Non-Linear Work*. Block Petrella Weisbord, 1991.

Meyers, C. *Improving Whole Systems: A Guidebook*. Block Petrella Weisbord, 1992.

Miller, L. *Barbarians to Bureaucrats: Corporate Life Cycle Strategies*. Fawcett Columbine, 1989.

Miller, L. M. *Design for Total Quality: A Workbook for Socio-Technical Design*. Miller Consulting Group, 1991a.

Miller, L. M. and Howard, J. *Managing Quality Through Teams.* Miller Consulting Group, 1991b.

Mintzberg, H. *Structure in Fives: Designing Effective Organizations.* Prentice Hall, 1993.

Mohrman, S. A. and Cummings, T. G. *Self-Designing Organizations.* Addison-Wesley, 1989.

Morgan, G. *Images of Organization.* Sage, 1986.

Morgan, G. *Imaginization.* Sage, 1993.

Nadler, D. and Tushman, M. *Strategic Organizational Design: Concepts, Tools, & Processes.* Harper Collins, 1988.

Nadler, D., Gerstein, M., Shaw, R. and associates. *Organizational Architecture: Designs Changing Organizations.* Jossey-Bass, 1992.

Pasmore, W. *Designing Effective Organizations: The Sociotechnical Systems Perspective.* Wiley 1988.

Robson, G. *Continuous Process Improvement: Simplifying Work Flow Systems.* The Free Press, 1991.

Rummler, G. A. and Brache, A. P. *Improving Performance.* Jossey-Bass, 1990.

Rummler, G. A. and Brache, A. P. "Managing the White Space," in the January 1991 issue of *Training.*

Terkel, S. *Working.* Avon Books, 1974.

Tomasko, R. *Rethinking the Corporation,* AMACOM, 1993.

Tyebjee, T., Bruno, A. and McIntyre, S. "Growing Ventures Can Anticipate Marketing Stages" in the January–February, 1983 issue of *Harvard Business Review.*

Woodward, H. and Buchholz, S. *Aftershock: Helping People Through Corporate Change.* Wiley 1987.

Index

A

Action plans: case study with, 228; drafting, 183–185; finalizing, 186–188; sequencing guidelines with, 185

Analysis, 24, 25–26; circumstances for performing, 26; factors in, 25; organization of, 27; parts of the system examined in, 8, 13; setting goals for the design using findings from, 128; training in tools and procedures of, 60. *See also* Environmental analysis; Human systems analysis; Technical processes analysis

Assessment, in human systems design, 168–172

Authority. *See* Lines of authority

Autonomy, and job design, 12, 17, 116, 164

B

Beckhard, R., 104

Beer, M., 185, 189

Block, P., 52

Boundaries: comparison of work process to, 104; process inputs and outputs with, 75

Brainstorming: defining desired outcomes and, 37; drafting action plans with, 184; identifying outsiders affected by structural change with, 108

Business environment, and setting goals and objectives for work processes, 64–66

Business environment matrix, 58; setting goals and objectives for work processes, 66; worksheet for, 64, 232

Business results, and defining desired outcomes, 36, 39

C

Case study, 195, 197–229

Champy, J., 133

Charter, design, 52

Charts: information-flow, 71, 137; job weaknesses, 117–118; responsibility, 104, 113, 115, 161, 221, 236–237; work-flow, 70, 78–79, 81, 97–98, 137

Checklist, gap verification, 55, 205–207

Compensation systems: drafting, 171. *See also* Reward systems

Conflict, and defining desired outcomes, 36

Consultant: finalizing the purpose and scope and, 52; role of, 51

Coordination mechanisms: analyzing structures and human resource systems and, 114; human structure and support systems including, 16, 25, 101, 149; human systems design for, 158–162, 176; identifying, 159–160; role of managers in new system and, 154

Cost reduction, and design improvements, 9

Cummings, T. G., 129, 131

Customers: analysis of environment and, 25, 26; defining desired outcomes and, 38; design and improved responsiveness to, 9; determining requirements and levels of satisfaction of, 60–63; identifying those who might be affected by structural change, 107–111; preliminary assessment and, 42, 43; process design and needs of, 10; role of, in design project, 51; setting goals and objectives for work processes and, 64; setting goals for the design and, 127; single point of contact for, 11; technical process and demands of, 15

Cycle time analysis, 90–94; case study of, 214; example of, 93–94; mapping alternative work flows with, 137; purpose of, 90; requirements for starting, 90; steps and specifics for, 92; when to use, 90; worksheet for, 70, 91, 92, 233–234

Cycle times, and design improvements, 9

D

Design, 24, 28–29; benefits of, 9; charter for, 52; choosing a process for, 132; drafting purpose and scope, 48; fragmented processes as symptom of lack of, 6; organization of, 29; requirements for starting, 28; risk in, 28; training in, 60; types of circumstances for starting, 28. *See also* Goal design; Human systems design; Technical process design

Desired outcomes worksheet, 77

Dillman, D., 58

E

Eisenstat, R. A., 185, 189

Eitington, J. E., 37

Environment: initiation and scoping and, 31; need for design due to conditions in, 6; as one part of system, 6, 13, 14; performance analysis of, 8, 13

Environmental analysis, 25, 57–66; determining customer requirements and levels of satisfaction in, 60–63; organization of, 57; prioritizing problems using, 120; results of, 58; setting goals for the design using, 126; setting goals and objectives for work processes in, 64–66; tools for, 58

F

Feedback: human systems design and, 168–172; values and norms reinforced by, 17. *See also* Intrinsic feedback

Flexibility, and design improvements, 9

Floor plans, 88–90

Flow of information. *See* Information flow

Flow of work. *See* Work flow

Flowcharts: case study work group process, 209–211; determining customer satisfaction, 62–63; determining process inputs and outputs, 76; establishing role of managers in new system, 156–157; output measures in a work flow, 145; setting design goals, 130; tryout assessment, 193; work flow for new process, 212–213

Focus group, in preliminary assessment, 42

Fragmentation, 3; business cost of, 4; defining desired outcomes and, 36; human cost of, 5; lack of design resulting in, 6

G

Galbraith, J., 114, 160

Gap verification checklist, 55, 205–207

Gaps, and preliminary assessment, 45

Goal design, 123–132; flowchart for, 130; organization of, 124; purpose of, 123; results of, 124; setting goals in, 126–130; verifying scope of design in, 131–132

Goals: analyzing business environment and setting, 64–66; designing work system and, 28; human systems design and, 169; role of managers in new system and, 154

Group process, definition of, 47

Group process skills, and job design, 166

H

Hackman, J. R., 105, 116, 164

Hammer, M., 133

Harris, R. T., 104

Human resource systems: analyzing, 112–115; human structure and support systems including, 17, 25, 101, 150

Human resources consultant, role of, 51

Human structure and support systems: designing work system and, 28; finalizing new design of, 176–177; initiation and scoping and, 31; need for design due to conditions in, 7; as one part of system, 6, 13, 16–17; performance analysis of, 8, 13

Maps: relationship, 70, 80–83, 97, 112, 113, 114, 137, 219; work space, 70

Matrixes: business environment, 58, 66, 232; identifying outsiders affected by structural change, 109, 111; preliminary assessment, 46, 204; problem definition, 121; skills and incentives, 104, 114, 115, 238; task/skill, 162, 167, 224–227

Meetings: brainstorming, 37; cycle time analysis with, 90; determining information flow, 84; drafting process descriptions, 95; drafting purpose and scope, 48, 49; establishing role of managers in new system and, 155; finalizing the purpose and scope, 52; finalizing the technical design, 146; finding problems with current technical process, 96; human systems analysis with, 103; human systems design with, 152; implementation with, 180, 184–185, 186–187, 188; predesign conference, 34; technical process analysis with, 69; technical process design with, 135

Michalko, M., 37

Miller, L. M., 72, 189

Mohrman, S. A., 131

N

Non-valued added activities, 11, 143

Norms. *See* Values and norms

O

Objectives setting, and analyzing business environment, 64–66

Oldham, G. R., 105, 116, 164

Organizational theory, and design, 8, 14

Outcome definition, 36–40; case study with, 200–203; documentation produced in, 40; drafting purpose and scope, 48; preliminary assessment using, 45; prioritizing problems and, 119; purpose of, 36; requirements for starting, 37; setting goals for the design using, 126, 129; steps and specifics for, 38–39; worksheet on, 77, 200–203; when to use, 36

Outputs from a process: designing new work flow with, 145; determining,

74–79; human systems design and, 169; work-flow chart of, 78–79

P

Performance, in defining desired outcomes, 38

Physical work flow, 87–90; designing a new work flow with, 144; floor plan diagrams in, 88–90; mapping alternative work flows with, 137; purpose of, 87; requirements for starting, 87; steps and specifics for, 87; when to use, 87

Predesign conference, 34

Preliminary assessment, 41–46; case study with, 204; determining customer requirements and levels of satisfaction using, 60; matrix for, 46, 204; purpose of, 41; requirements for starting, 42; setting goals and objectives for work processes and, 64; steps and specifics for, 43–45; when to use, 41

Problem prioritization, 119–121; matrix for, 121; purpose of, 119; requirements for starting, 119; steps and specifics for, 119–120; when to use, 119

Process descriptions: drafting, 95; steps and specifics for, 95

Process design, 10, 11; determining process inputs and outputs and, 74; training in, 60

Process improvement, and design, 8

Process inputs and outputs, determining, 74–79

Process parameters worksheet, 215–217

Product and service requirements, 15; human systems design and, 169; technical process analysis and, 25, 67, 133

Products: list state-changes to, 71; records on, 72

Purpose of design project: drafting, 47–51; finalizing, 52–55

Q

Quality of work life: setting goals for the design using, 128–129; defining desired outcomes and, 36, 39; preliminary assessment and, 44–45; role of managers in new system and, 154